2502

BOOKS BY ROBERT BRINGHURST

POETRY

The Shipwright's Log • 1972
Cadastre • 1973
Bergschrund • 1975
Tzuhalem's Mountain • 1982
The Beauty of the Weapons: Selected Poems 1972–82 • 1982
Tending the Fire • 1985
The Blue Roofs of Japan • 1986
Pieces of Map, Pieces of Music • 1986
Conversations with a Toad • 1987
New World Suite nº 3 • 1995
The Calling: Selected Poems 1970–1995 • 1995

PROSE

Visions: Contemporary Art in Canada (with Geoffrey James,
    Russell Keziere & Doris Shadbolt) • 1983
Ocean/Paper/Stone • 1984
The Raven Steals the Light (with Bill Reid) • 1984
The Black Canoe: Bill Reid and the Spirit of Haida Gwaii
    (with Ulli Steltzer) • 1991
The Elements of Typographic Style • 1992

ROBERT BRINGHURST

THE *Calling*

Selected Poems 1970–1995

M&S

THE MODERN CANADIAN POETS SERIES

Canadian Cataloguing in Publication Data

Bringhurst, Robert, 1946–
The calling : selected poems, 1970–1995

(The Modern Canadian poets)
Includes bibliographical references and index.
ISBN 0-7710-1651-4

I. Title. II. Series.

PS8553.R5C3 1995   C811'.54   C94-932662-3
PR9199.3.B75C3 1995

The publishers acknowledge the support of the Canada Council
and the Ontario Arts Council for its publishing program.

Printed and bound in Canada on acid-free paper

McClelland & Stewart Inc.
The Canadian Publishers
481 University Avenue
Toronto, Ontario
M5G 2E9

1 2 3 4 5 · 99 98 97 96 95

Φημίωι, ὅς ῥ’ ἤειδε παρὰ μνηστῆρσιν ἀνάγκηι

Gam hau hla guudangangghi suuganggangga.
Sghaana qidas tsiiyahlingaay gaawun diigi suuwus.
Ghaagaanhau hl suuwugangga.

CONTENTS

Years ago in a Bosnian town a woman tried repeatedly to speak to me, though the words she knew and trusted were words I did not understand. At length, in desperation, she gave me an egg. So I was present at the birth of language – as all of us are many times in our lives. I saw a gesture turn an egg, for just an instant and for eternity, into a noun, and the egg transform the gesture into a verb. I have known since that moment that I wanted – no matter how preposterous and impossible it might be – to learn all the words and grammars in the world, and that poetry nevertheless precedes them all and can make its way, if it must, with the help of none. The egg is gone now, and Bosnia, like Auschwitz, is a permanent cry of pain – far less a legacy from the past, it seems to me, than a curse on the future, delivered and witnessed by us. Yet the gift remains: a feast to last a lifetime, made from a single egg, which was not consumed.

If these are poems, then the words they contain have been turned momentarily into something *outside language* – something as simple and inexplicable as eggs – so they can be given, like eggs; and they must be given, because only then can they turn, on the other side of the silence, back into words – just as a word, the only noun in an *ad hoc* language, once retransformed itself into an egg in the nest of my hand.

When and wherever the poems turn back into words, I cannot know what they will say. It is true of course that I publish and perform them for the sake of what we call communication. But I made them for reasons more urgent and private than that. Like the twitter of bats, the chatter of oilbirds and the clucking and moaning of dolphins, they began as tuneless and investigative songs: as desperate attempts at echolocation. Those who imagine that bats and birds have nothing to say may therefore take the view that I have nothing to say either.

I would rather, of course, say nothing. I would rather any book, especially a book of poems, be an act of speaking more than of writing, but I would rather the speaking were done by the poems themselves, or by the voices in the poems, and not by me. Let them do the speaking, and let me take dictation, edit, translate, and do literary housework – which is all that the *writing* of poetry is. Behind that, in the world of bats and birds and human beings, sometimes there is silence, and sometimes there is being calling out to itself in the hope that being is listening. Writing, if it lives, is rooted in speaking, and speaking, if it lives, is rooted in listening for the speech, the calling, of being. There, I think, is where the real work of poetry occurs.

Ten years ago, I made my first attempts at layering the voices: making poems like polyphonic music, in which several speakers speak at the same time though they have different things to say. Again, I was trying to ask where I was and record what I heard. But learning to hear and learning to speak go hand in hand, and I found I could learn far more in this regard from composers of madrigals, motets and string quartets than from other writers, including those who write for the stage. Several unsophisticated examples of this chamber music for speaking voices are included in this book, though only one, the *New World Suite nº 3*, for three voices, is printed in full score.

There is not much doubt that writing in multiple voices causes extra work for readers. Whether it yields anything useful in return, each reader must decide. To me, the method has become essential, both as a metaphor for the cultural plurality of the world in which I live, and as a means of second-guessing and contradicting myself without delay.

I hope, of course, that these polyphonic poems, like the others, will be freed from the prison of silence now and again. Poems live in the voice, not in the eye – with whatever intonations, emendations, repetitions or deletions are chosen by the one who sets them free. But for the poems with several voices, friends are also indispensable. One reader or speaker at once is not enough.

In many of the poems, the voices of the dead are also quoted or evoked. The dead, in my experience, are indispensable too, especially when they are silent, watching and listening as they do in the land, the air and us. I don't suppose the dead are reading books, yet they seem present far more palpably in books, where we read them, than they do in magazine racks or in stadiums, gymnasiums and classrooms, where the living crowd them out. Some books, at any rate, seem able to desegregate the living and the dead – and that is the only kind of book I have ever wanted to read or write.

At the beginning of this book, there are two short epigraphs or talismans – two tiny medicine bundles of words. The first is a line from the *Odyssey*. It remembers another poet, "Phemios, forced to sing for the suitors" – one of the poem's most minor characters, but a portrait of the artist in our time. The second quotation comes from an oral poet in another great but less widely taught tradition. It comes from the only surviving fragment of a poem spoken in Haida in the winter of 1900 by Job Moody of the Sttawaas Xhaaydaghaay, transcribed by a linguist named John Swanton. The subject of the poem was the creation and arrangement of the world. In these lines, the Loon speaks to Voicehandler, the Raven's father's father, while the earth still lies beneath the flood. The Loon has been going out repeatedly and calling, then coming back to the house. The old man finally asks the reason, and the Loon says:

Gam hau hla guudangangghi suuganggangga.
Sghaana qidas tsiiyahlingaay gaawun diigi suuwus.
Ghaagaanhau hl suuwugangga.

I am not speaking only from my own mind.
The gods tell me they need places to live.
That is the reason I am speaking.

The flood Job Moody and other survivors of the Haida holocaust spoke of in their poems was made of water, but the one that they confronted in their daily lives, and that now confronts us all, is made of something else. It is made, in fact, of us – and of course, of our machines and the wastes and effluents, tailing ponds and junkheaps, hydro dams and factories, parking lots, highways and clearcuts that come in our wake. It is made of words, numbers, equations, explanations, interpretations, ingenious ideas and connections – some of them perhaps as essential and lovely as water, in modest quantities, and just as destructive as water when they overflow their banks.

While Odysseus was out having epic adventures, Penelope also suffered a flood of ambitious advances. Suitors are something few households and perhaps no culture can afford to do entirely without, and they might, under certain constraints and conditions, be welcome. But for Penelope, as for the earth, the flood that promises renewal becomes a plague instead. The Haida poet Job Moody saw that plague, that flood, at one of its heights, and he heard rebirth in the loon's call even so. That too, I think, is a kind of echolocation. It is being calling out to itself, in the hope that being is listening.

I imagine no more than a spindrift of language, a planktonic bloom of thought, on the surface of the flood, instead of anything so fancy and consoling as an ark. And beneath the flood, a lot of homeless gods – who dream of alpine meadows, rivers, rocks and trees and coral reefs and coves – forced to make do for a time with a diet that might consist of little more than sterile earth and poisoned air and water. And a question, posed in an unknown language, by a bird who never came aboard the boat.

Bowen Island, British Columbia · 1995

☐   CONVERSATIONS WITH A TOAD

I

Not for the toad, no, but for us,
>   In this poem a man talks
as a prologue only: two
>   to a toad. The toad may listen
legends. One. That a three-legged
>   or he may not. That, perhaps,
crow with vermilion feathers
>   is not the man's concern.
nests in the sun; in the restless
>   I suppose it is not the toad's concern
moon, a rabbit, a willow tree, a toad.
>   either. I am convinced, though,
Two. *Near water, a rock. Where a toad*
>   that the silences of the toad
had been sitting, an old woman sits.
>   are the most important – I mean
She is deaf, dumb and blind. But she hears
>   the most meaningful – parts of the poem,
through the soles of her feet, speaks
>   filling the dark shells
from under her skirt, and sees
>   of the man's ears and the spaces
through the holes in the palms of her hands.
>   between his sentences,

What do they mean, these
>   filling his syllables, filling the wrinkled,
images? I cannot tell you.
>   stretched and invisible skins of his words,
I learned them here and there
>   filling his eyes wherever he looks
among the Tsimshian and the immigrants –
>   and his lungs whenever he breathes.

Celts and Chinese – who don't know
                    So the silences of the toad would appear
anything anymore except whatever it is
                    to be nothing but empty space
that everybody knows, and how
                    if the poem were printed, but
to keep silent –

who carry their other knowledge
                    the man in the poem would not know
shrivelled into undeciphered images,
                    how to speak it without them.
symbols, souvenirs. I lied then, didn't I,
                    In this poem a man talks
when I said these legends were for us?
                    to a toad. He tries, at first,
They don't have much to do
                    talking to us, but not very hard.
with us, with me, with you. They are true
                    It seems that he really wants
stories. I should, instead,
                    to talk to the toad instead.
have told them to the toad.
                    And so he does.

II

So few bones, toad, you must know
how to count them and give them away.
You can swallow your own skin, and pluck dinner,
still living, out of the air without lifting a hand.
And you let in the weather, taking
your temperature from the world.

A toothless carnivore, an unarmed hunter. Your tongue
hinged at the lip like a swallowed reflection.
Like one who in preference to speaking
is spoken. Like one who *uneats*
bits of the world – or the whole world: whatever
is already eaten. Who unthinks what others have thought,
unreads what is read, unwrites what is written.

Nevertheless, toad, like us, you have traded
a tail for elbows and pelvis and fingers
and toes, and one mouth for another, the smooth
for the angular: traded the long
hug of the water for the abstemious,
pontifical kiss of the air.

III

Behind you: the owl, whose eyes
have no corners: the owl with her quick
neck, who faces whatever she sees.
The raven, with voices like musselshell, wellwater, wood.
The dippers with voices like water on water.
The ruffed grouse drumming in the Douglas-fir.
And the heron flying in whole notes,
the kingfisher crossing in dotted eighths
and in quarters – both silent; much later,
two voices like washboards:
one bass, coarser than gravel,
one mezzo, crushed gravel and sand.

Their beauty bites into the truth.
One way to fail to be is to be merely
pretty. But that beauty: it feeds on you; we
feed on it. As you feed on this
moth, toad, or may: he may yet be
your dinner: his hazelnut tonsure,

the face like a goat's but clean,
and the mane like brown cornsilk.
Nerves spring from his forehead like fernfronds,
like feathers. He too is transformed.
This is the last life, toad.
Those who eat will be eaten. That
is the one resurrection.

We who kill not to eat but to mark
our domain – to build and breed, in place
of what is, what we choose to create –
have reduced by that much the population of heaven.

IV

The mind is the other. The mind
is a long complication of water. The mind
is time, space and all creatures. The mind
is the world. What we keep in the head,
with its dark facets, this jewel,
is a small, disproportional model.

What we are not is all we can think with.
In the leaking cup of the skull
we dip up the other. Daily we trade it
for money, for comfort, for power. But what we are not
is all we can think with. To hold and let go
is all we can do with whatever we are.

V

My people no longer stare into water
and fire for clues to the future. We no longer
read even the signs in our faces and hands.
Instead we grind lenses and mirrors

to sop up the spilled light of the stars. We decipher
the rocks that we walk on, too, while we loot them.

Toad, as we level the future we make
topographical maps of the past.

But the mirrors say at the edges
of what we can see, things are leaving
and taking their light with them, flying away
at six hundred million miles an hour –
or were when the light that is reaching us now
was just leaving them, ten billion years ago.

Ten billion years seems
long to us, toad, though to you
it is little: a few dozen times
the age of your ancestors' graves
in these rocks. Only two or three times
the age of the oldest rocks we have found.

What is is too quick for our fingers
and tongues to keep up with. The light
outmanoeuvres us. Time and space close over us, toad.
The lock of the sky will turn but not open.
We are where we are and have been here
forever. Longer, that is, than we can remember.

VI

Your ancestors, toad, were kings
in a world of trilobites, fish, bryozoans.
Do you know any stories, toad, of a species
determined, as mine is, to cease to have meaning?
Is it really so onerous, toad, to live
and to die at less distance from being?

My people have named a million species of insects.
They tell me that millions more are unnamed –
tens of millions among the living
and hundreds of millions among the dead.

It is good news, toad: that no one can list
what exists in the world. But not good enough.
Named or unnamed, if it lives, we can kill it.
We owe to the stones
that many chances and that many means
to kill us.

In the blank rock of Precambrian time
the earliest creatures, too soft to leave fossils,
too light to leave footprints, have left us
old proteins and sugars as signatures. We will leave
chronicles filled with our griefs and achievements,
a poetry spoken by locusts as they descend.

VII

Woodlice breed in the fallen alder.
Toad, the varied thrush is a beautiful bird.
And the red-shafted flickers, who feed there.
Uses will form for us too in the end.

What is is the truth. What precedes it
is meaning. We will not destroy
being, toad. We will not. But I think
we will overreligiously clean it.

Yet the voices still seep through us too. Even
through us, who have long since forgotten:
to pray does not mean to send messages
to the gods; to pray means to listen.

VIII

We have barely stopped binding the feet
of the women, toad. Is it true we ought to be binding
the hands of the men? Or weighting them
back into frequent touch with the ground?
Like eyes, the hands open and close, squeeze and release.
The feet, like the ears, are always wide open.

Toad, on the rocks near the stream
are the pictures of dreamers, and where the head
of the dreamer should be, there is a summary
of the dream. Close your eyes, say the rocks,
and dream of things seen in the darkness.
Open your eyes and dream of the sun.

The mind is a body, with shinbones and wrists
and roots, milkteeth and wings,
ankles and petals, fins,
feathers and dewclaws, leafstalks and lungs.
It is larva, pupa, imago, sea urchin,
tree. Ripening ideas drop from its limbs.

IX

Toad, all the roads from a man to a woman,
a man to a man, woman to man, woman to woman
lead through the nonhuman. This
is the reason, toad, for musicians.
                    In this poem a man talks
We speak to each other by means
                    to a toad. The toad may listen
of the bones and the horns and the bodies
                    or he may not. That
and bowels of dead animals, plucking
                    is not the man's concern.

their gutstrings, thumping their bellies, plinking
                    I suppose it is not the toad's concern
their evened teeth laid out in a row.
                    either. I believe,
The animals give us our speech and the means
                    nevertheless, that the silences
of our thinking, just as the dreamers'
                    of the toad are the most important –
masks open the doors of our dreams.
                    I mean the most meaningful –
The voice is a face. The face is a vision.
                    parts of the poem.

                    How could the man in the poem find
                    his own silence without them?

        X

In winter the mountain goats think.
In summer they gather. Thought
equals solitude. Toad, is there no other
answer? Thought is the mind walking
the ridges and edges of being, not
the tuned instruments crooning their perfect routines.

That smoothness is blasphemy. Thought
is the mute breaking through in the voice.
Like ice going out in the spring,
the voice giving way.
The language dug up by the roots
where thought has been speaking.

Leap, toad. Our invincible
greed, a dead silence, an absolute
absence of meaning, is closing.

□   HUNTERS & PILGRIMS

*Zichan answered: When spiritual beings have a place
to return to, they need not become malicious.
I have allowed them a place to return to.*

Zuǒqiu Míng
Zuǒ Zhuàn

Han vilde læse sit Fader vor,
men hand kunde kun huske den store Tabel.

*He wanted to say his prayer, but could remember
nothing but the multiplication table.*

Hans Christian Andersen
Sneedronningen

THE BEAUTY OF THE WEAPONS

El-Arish, 1967

A long-armed man can
carry the nine-millimetre
automatic gun slung
backward over the right shoulder.

With the truncated butt
caught in the cocked
elbow, the trigger
falls exactly to hand.

These things I remember,
and a fuel-pump gasket cut
from one of the innumerable
gas masks in the roadside dump.

I bring back manuscript picked
up around incinerated trucks
and notes tacked next
to automatic track controls.

Fruits of the excavation.
This is our archaeology.
A dig in the debris
of a civilization six weeks old.

The paper is crisp and brittle
with the dry rock and the weather.
The Arabic is brittle
with the students' first exposure

to air-war technology and speed.
Ridiculous to say so, but
the thought occurs,
that Descartes would be pleased:

the calculus is the language
of the latest Palestinian
disputations
in the field of theology.

The satisfying feel
of the fast traverse
on the anti-aircraft guns
is not in the notes.

It lies latent and cool
in the steel, like the intricate
mathematics
incarnate in the radar:

the antennae folded and rolled
like a soldier's tent,
sweeping the empty
sky and the barren horizon,

the azimuth and the elevation,
sweeping the empty air
into naked abstraction,
leading the guns.

The signal is swirled until it
flies over the lip like
white, weightless
wine from a canteen cup.

Invisibly, the mechanism sings.
It sings. It sings like a six-ton flute:
east, west, always the same
note stuck in the rivetless throat.

A silent song as intricate
as any composition by Varèse,
and seeming, for the moment, far
more beautiful, because,

to us, more deadly.
Therefore purer, more
private, more familiar,
more readily feared, or desired:

a dark beauty with a steel sheen,
caught in the cocked
mind's eye and brought
down with an extension of the hand.

SONG OF THE SUMMIT

The difference is nothing you can see – only
the dressed edge of the air
over those stones, and the air goes

deeper into the lung, like a long fang,
clean as magnesium. Breathing
always hollows out a basin,

leaving nothing in the blood
except an empty
cup, usable for drinking

anything the minds finds – bitter
light or bright darkness or the cold
corner of immeasurable distance.

This is what remains: the pitted blood
out looking for the vein,
tasting of the tempered tooth and the vanished flame.

ARARAT

The deepening scour of the keel across this
granular water. Nothing more. The fissure
through the estuary five
thousand feet over the headwater. These
are the real mouths of rivers: the teeth,
not the slough and the rattles.

We have been here
before, eating raw air, but have always
forgotten,

all day eating the air the light
impales,
stalking the singular animal –

I no longer remember whether a fish
or a bird. Nor whether its song or its silence
is what we were listening for. I remember
a bow in a black tree, and a snowbound
ploughshare.
Here is no spoor and no flotsam
timber. Simply the blue sliding into
the furrow on the tilting light, and the violet
sky always casting the same white shadow.

A QUADRATIC EQUATION

Voice: the breath's tooth.
Thought: the brain's bone.
Birdsong: an extension
of the beak. Speech:
the antler of the mind.

THE GREENLAND STONE

Gods immersed in the masked
North American air
vanish like cryolite,
vanish like the kayak's
white stone anchor hitting
bright blue arctic water.

The snowfall in the stone
clears when the lightfall slows,
the way the heart's thought, the eye's
mossy chalcedony
and the mind's wet marrow
clarify when it quickens.

POEM ABOUT CRYSTAL

Look at it, stare
into the crystal because
it will tell you, not
the future, no, but
the quality of crystal,
clarity's nature,
teach you the stricture
of uncut, utterly
uncluttered light.

A LESSON IN BOTANY

Consider it: in the mountains
of Malaya, on the mammoth grape:
the masterpiece, a 24-pound
flower, its diameter
28 inches in full bloom.
A triumph! Leafless, asepalous,
rootless and stemless: pure flower.

Its adhesive seeds grow
tendrils into the Tetrastigma
vine. It takes nine months to open
fully and stays open seven days.
It has five petals, reddish
brown and often mottled. All
its organs are dead-center
in a blood-coloured, lidded cup.

Consider, furthermore, its smell,
which is precisely that of
24 fully opened
pounds of rotting meat; the method
of its pollination: carrion-
eating flies; and of its seed
dissemination: fruit rats.

Sir Thomas Stamford Raffles,
the man who planted the Union
Jack on Singapore, has given it
its name: it is *Rafflesia*
arnoldi. This, of course,
is history. *Rafflesia*
arnoldi by any other
name would be *Rafflesia*
arnoldi as we know it and
the largest flower in the natural world.

SOME CIPHERS

If I say
$1 + e^{\pi i} = 0,$
I have recorded a rather
elaborate but arguably beautiful way
of reducing unity to zero.

If however I say
$1 + 1 = 2$, or 1
$+ 1 = 1$, I have made a concrete
assertion having to do
with construction or fusion.

Observe, now, that on certain occasions
$1 + 1 \to 0$. The formula
$1 + x = 0$, where x
may equal, for instance, $e^{\pi i}$,
may then be of more interest.

Consider, further, $1 = 0$.
This, in mathematical terms, may be called
cancellation. It differs from $0 = 1$,
which may, in mathematical terms, be called
the creation *ex nihil* of number, or,

in nonmathematical terms, the invention
of terror.
Consider, therefore, $0 \neq$
0, or $0 = x$, where x
is not equal to zero. Climb left through the zero

and watch, looking back at
the blood in its jacket,
the breath in its jacket,
the absence
opening its arms.

The squid is in fact
a carnivorous pocket
containing a pen, which serves
the squid as his skeleton.

The squid is a raised finger or
an opposed thumb. The squid's quill
is his long, scrupulous nail, which
is invisible.

The squid is a short-beaked
bird who has eaten
his single wing, or impaled
himself on his feather.

The squid, however,
despite his Cadurcian
wineskin and 400 cups,
does not entertain.

The squid, with his eight
arms and his two
brushes and his sepia,
does not draw.

The squid knows too that the use
of pen and ink is neither recording
impressions nor signing his name
to forms and petitions.

But the squid may be said,
for instance, to transcribe
his silence into the space
between seafloor and wave,

or to invoke an unspoken
word, whose muscular
nonpronunciation the squid
alone is known to have mastered.

The squid carries his ink
in a sack, not a bottle.
With it the squid makes
artifacts.

These are mistakable for
portraiture, or
for self-portraiture, or,
to the eyes of the squid-eating whale,

for the squid, who in the meanwhile grows
transparent and withdraws,
leaving behind him his
coagulating shadows.

□ DEUTERONOMY

And Joseph took them both, Ephraim in his right hand toward Israel's left hand, and Manasseh in his left hand toward Israel's right hand, and brought them near unto him. And Israel stretched out his right hand and laid it upon Ephraim's head, who was the younger, and his left hand upon Manasseh's head, guiding his hands willingly.... And Joseph said unto his father, Not so, my father: for this is the firstborn; put thy right hand upon his head. And his father refused, and said, I know it, my son, I know it: he also....

And the Lord thy God shall circumcise thine heart, and the heart of thy seed....

Genesis xlviii / Deuteronomy xxx

for Roo Borson & Joseph Keller

What I am I have stolen.
I have climbed the mountain with nothing in my hand
except the mountain. I have spoken to the god
with nothing in my hand except my other hand.
One against the other, the smith against the wizard,
I have watched them. I have watched them
wrestle one another to the ground.
I have watched my body carry my head around
like a lamp, looking for light among the broken stones.

What I am I have stolen.
Even the ingrained web
in the outstretched palm of this body,
limping on oracle-finger and thumb,
dragging a great weight, an arm or a tail
like the wake of a boat drug over the ground.
What I am I have stolen. Even my name.

My brother, I would touch you, but these
are your hands. Yours, yours, though I call them
my own. My brother, I would hold your shoulders,
but only the voice is mine. My brother,
the head is a hand that does not open
and the face is full of claws.

What I am I have stolen.
These mountains which were never mine
year after year have remade me.
I have seen the sky coloured with laughter.
I have seen the rocks between the withered water
and the quaking light. I have climbed the mountain

with nothing in my hand except the handholds
as I came upon them, leaving my hands behind.

I have eaten the sun, it is my muscle,
eaten the moon, it is my bone.
I have listened to the wind, whipped
in the heart's cup, slap and whistle in the vein.

My father said:
the wood will crawl into the apple,
the root will crawl into the petal,
the limb will crawl into the sepal
and hide.
But the fruit has eaten the tree, has eaten the flower.
The body, which is flower and fruit together,
has swallowed its mother, root and stem.
The lungs are leaves and mine are golden.

I have seen the crow carry the moon
against the mountain.
I have seen the sky crawl under a stone.

I have seen my daughter
carried on the land's shoulder.
I have seen the wind change
colour above her.
I have lain in silence, my mouth to the ground.

I have seen the light drop
like a wagon-sprag in the crisp stubble.
I have seen the moon's wheels
jounce through the frozen ruts
and chirp against the pebbles.
I have seen the metal angels
clatter up and down.

I have seen the flushed ewes
churn in the pen and picked rams boil
against the hazel. I have seen them
strip the poplar, scrub the buckeye bare.
I have seen the mixed flocks
flow through the scented hills like braided oil.
I who never moved as they do.
I have climbed the mountain
one foot up and one hoof down.

The breath is a bone the flesh comes loose around.

Flower and fruit together.
But this other, this other
who is always in the body,
lungs in the belly, head
between the thighs.
O his arms go
backward, and his legs go
side to side.

My son, you have asked for a blessing. I give you
this blessing. I tell you,

the eye will flow out of the socket like water,
the ear will gore like a horn
and the tongue like another,
the sailor will stay in his house near the harbour,
the laborer, blinkered and fed, will stay at his labour,
the soldier will soldier,
the lawyer will smile like milk and swill liquor,
the judge will glide like a snake keeping pace with the horses,
the man with gay eyes will like chocolate,
the roebuck will wrestle the air and you will hear music,
the rancher will prosper,
the wolf will walk out of your hand and his teeth will be shining.

But this one, my grandson, the young one,
this one will steal
the sun and the moon, the eye and the tooth
of the mountain. This one will ride with his dogs
through the galleries of vision. This one will move
among the rain-worn shapes of men
with faces in his hands and the fingers writhing.
This one will slide his spade through the sea
and come away carrying wheat and linen.

This one, the young one, how tall,
shaking hands and trading armor
with his dark-eyed brother.

My son, you must do more
than listen to the angel; you must wrestle him.
And one thing further: he must be there.
The muscle in the air, the taut light
hinged in the milky gristle
and the swollen dark, the smell
like the smell of a cornered animal.

I have oiled these stones to sharpen the wind.
I have come or I have gone, I have forgotten.
I hold what I hold
in this chiasma of the hands.

I have set my ear against the stone
and heard it twirling.
I have set my teeth against the stone
and someone said he heard it singing.

AN AUGURY

The raven preceded the dove
out of the ark and for seven days circled
water, waiting for a perch, and for seven more
circled, waiting for the dove.

ESSAY ON ADAM

There are five possibilities. One: Adam fell.
Two: he was pushed. Three: he jumped. Four:
he only looked over the edge, and one look silenced him.
Five: nothing worth mentioning happened to Adam.

The first, that he fell, is too simple. The fourth,
fear, we have tried. It is useless. The fifth,
nothing happened, is dull. The choices are these:
he jumped or was pushed. And the difference between them

is only an issue of whether the demons
work from the inside out or from the outside
in: the one
theological question.

The bush. Yes. It burned like they say it did.
Lit up like an oak in October – except
that there is no October in Egypt. Voices
came at me and told me to take off my shoes,
and I did that. That desert is full of men's shoes.
And the flame screamed, *I am what I am.*
I am whatever it is that is me,
and nothing can but something needs to be
done about it. If anyone asks,
all you can say is, What is is what sent me.

I went. But I brought my brother to do
the talking, and I did the tricks – the Nile
full of fishguts and frogs, the air opaque
and tight as a scab, the white-hot hail,
and boils, and bugs, and when nothing had worked right,
we killed them and ran. We robbed them of every
goddamned thing we could get at and carry
and took off, and got through the marsh at low tide
with the wind right, and into the desert. The animals
died, of course, but we kept moving.

Abraham came up easy. We took
the unknown road and ate hoarfrost and used
a volcano for a compass. I had no plan.
We went toward the mountains. I wanted, always,
to die in the mountains, not in that delta.
And not in a boat, at night, in swollen water.
We travelled over dead rock and drank dead water,
and the hoarfrost wasn't exactly hoarfrost.
They claimed it tasted like coriander,
but no two men are agreed on the taste
of coriander. Anyway,
we ate it. And from time to time we caught quail.

Men and half-men and women, we marched
and plodded into those hills, and they exploded
into labyrinths of slag. The air licked us
like a hot tongue, twisting and flapping and gurgling
through the smoke like men suffocating or drowning, saying,
An eye for an eye, and on certain occasions
two eyes for one eye. Either way, you model me
in thin air or unwritten words, not in wood,
not in metal. I am gone from the metal when the metal
hits the mould. You will not get me into any image
that will not move when I move, and move
with my fluency. Moses! Come up!

I went. But I wore my shoes and took a waterskin.
I climbed all day, with the dust eating holes
in my coat and choking me, and the rock cooking me.
What I found was a couple of flat stones
marked up as if the mountain had written all over them.
I was up there a week, working to cool them,
hungry and sweating and unable to make sense of them,
and I fell coming down and broke both of them.
Topping it all, I found everybody down there drooling
over Aaron's cheap figures, and Aaron chortling.

I went up again to get new stones,
and the voices took after me that time and threw me
up between the rocks and said I could see them.
They were right. I could see them. I was standing right
behind them,
and I saw them. I saw the mask's insides,
and what I saw is what I have always seen.
I saw the fire, and it flowed, and it was moving away
and not up into me. I saw *nothing,*
and it was widening all the way around me.
I collected two flat stones, and I cut them
so they said what it seemed to me two stones
should say, and I brought them down without dropping them.

The blisters must have doubled my size, and Aaron said
I almost glowed in the dark when I got down.
Even so, it seemed I was pulling my stunts
more often then than in Egypt. I had to,
to hold them. They had to be led to new land,
and all of them full of crackpot proverbs and cockeyed
ideas about directions. Aaron and I
outbellowed them day after day, and in spite of it
they died. Some of weakness, certainly, but so many of them
died of being strong. The children stood up to it
best, out of knowing no different – but with no
idea what to do with a ploughshare, no
idea what a river is. What could they do
if they got there? What can they even know how to wish for?
I promised them pasture, apple trees, cedar,
waterfalls, snow in the hills, sweetwater
wells instead of these arroyos, wild grapes....

Words. And whatever way I say them, words only.
I no longer know why I say them, even though
the children like hearing them. They come when I call them,
and their eyes are bright, but the light in them is empty.
It is too clear. It contains ... the clarity only.
But they come when I call to them. Once I used to sing them
a song about an eagle and a stone, and each time
I sang it, somehow the song seemed changed,
and the words drifted into the sunlight. I do not
remember the song now, but I remember
that I sang it, and the song was the law, and the law
was the song. The law is a song, I am certain....
And I climbed to the head of this canyon. They said
I could look down at the new land
if I sat here, and I think it is so, but my eyes
are no longer strong, and I am tired now of looking.

☐ THE OLD IN THEIR KNOWING

They saw moreover that the whole physical world was in motion, with nothing coming true from its continuous transformation, and they decided that nothing at all could be truthfully said about something that was always and everywhere changing. From these conclusions stem the more extreme views of some who claimed to out-Herakleitos Herakleitos. Take Kratylos for example. Finally he stopped talking altogether and only moved his finger. And he censured Herakleitos for saying one could not step twice into the same river. His own view was that one could not do so even once.

Aristotle, *Metaphysics* 1010a

1

Herakleitos says a dry soul is wisest and best.
Herakleitos is undeniably
right in these matters. These
bright tatters of wisdom, cast
over grey welter and spume should at any rate yield
a few visions and reflections, a little light
cutting crosswise like a fin,
splayed against the sea's grain
or annealed on the wave crest.

A dry soul. Dry: that is to say
kiln-dried, cured like good lumber or old Bordeaux,
salt-pork and pemmican, meat of the soul
under the chokecherry,
                              sunlight
and sea salt arrayed in the grain.

2

Herakleitos says something of concord – not
like a carpenter's clamp or lashed
logs, as in Homer.
Harmony with an arched back,
laminated ash upended like an unlaid keel, the curl
of live flesh in the fire, flexed
like the soul between the muscle and the bone, like
the bow, like the lyre.

3

All things are exchangeable for
fire and fire for all things,
like gold for goods and goods for gold,
or so sings old
                    Herakleitos.

4

Dead men are gods; men are dead gods, said
Herakleitos. Immortals are mortal, mortals immortal.
The birth of the one is the death of the other;
the dying of one gives life to the other.

The living are dying. The dead live forever,
except when the living disturb them, and this
they must do. The gods die
when men live forever. Air, earth and fire
die too. Dying, we mother and sire

the other: our only and own
incarnation.

5

Wind stirs his ashes.

for J. Michael Yates

Parmenides was no fool. Parmenides
knew that the coast of Campania
wasn't the Aegean's east rim,
that it wasn't Phokaia,
and the rich holes of Calabria,
regardless Pythagoras,
were dust-bins in comparison
to Miletos.

Larger, yes, to be sure.
The great frontier. The Tyrrhene waves were
strangely like Texas,
and the sheer
size of it all may have got to him.

Parmenides talked,
and Parmenides was capable of observing
that his voice drained off under the outsized rocks,
and his dreams were pale
like pyrites, or paler, like the gangue
milled away from Ionian metal.

Thirty-odd years, and thirty lines wasted
on wagon axles, door hinges, horses, veils
and the sun's girls, and suddenly
then
Parmenides
hummed to himself, caught an idea clean
in his teeth and bit into it, singing:

... things that appear to be,
even though they all exist, actually
have to be there
always. Everywhere.

And Parmenides lay in the goat-dunged, heavy-stemmed
grass, imagining things and thinking
of all of them *there* in the inwoven ply, his mind flying
and gulping, trying for the whole cascade:
his brainlobes pumping like lungs, like a muscle,
the nervecords thundering in the bones' coulisses,
and the heart's whole cargo coming
tumbling up into him:
goddesses, girls, white water, olive trees,
sharks' roe, the sea haze,
the migrating eye of the flounder

... have to be there
always. Everywhere.

And this revelation
distressed and dumbfounded
Parmenides.
Nevertheless he pushed into it,
choked on exhaustion, swallowed, piled into it:
the whole bill of lading,
everything intermingling into

finally, only
the endless, full,
indivisible stillness:
the lock
on the safe of creation.

Parmenides then took up law
and wrote numerous statutes,
a very great number of statutes
which, Plutarch reports,
were enforced for some years in Elea.

III   MILETOS

One looked down and the other looked around
when Anaximander and Anaximenes
learned their master Thales
had been drowned.

IV   A SHORT HISTORY

"And he talks of time," said Hippolytus,
 the fat-headed presbyter,
 of Anaximander, Milesian
 sage, then nine centuries dead.

What Anaximander in fact says is,
The necessity is
that things flare out into that out of which
they came to be, because

they pay one another the penalty
and compensation for
the mutual injustice of their
chronological order.

Anaximander does not talk of time.
He lays open the way for
Anaximenes' love of the live air
as a bluer arcanum.

V EMPEDOKLES: SEVEN FRAGMENTS

1

Maxillae went into motion without mandibles,
arms walked naked, unhinged from their shoulders,
eyeballs wandered without brows....

2

A lot of them sprouted sternums and eyes on both sides.
Ungulates with human faces, also the opposite,
ox-headed bipeds, appeared. Other mixtures: creatures
part man and part woman, with umbrous, broadleaved limbs.

3

This is how the fire, as it separated, germinated
the night-flowering seedlings of human beings. Listen.
Crooked forms imprinted out of air existed first. They
were partly water and partly opaque shape. Fire
desired to arrive at its own image, therefore fire
forced them into flower. They didn't yet have attractive limbs,
nor the hand and the lonely voice that fuse in a man.

4

… tumbling in the surf and undertow
of blood, where the thing called thought is. Thought
is, in fact, the blood around the beating heart.

5

… sighting in on the peaks, one after the other, and not just
talking one straight trail through the understory words.

6

There is an instrument of mandamus, an edict issued
long ago by the gods. It does not expire. It is sealed
edge to edge with promises. It says that whenever
one of the demons who are doomed to immortality hexes
his hands, commits a murder or perjury, he is to be
banished for three hundred centuries. He is to be born
into mortal bodies, exiled from happiness, inhabiting
one incarnation of pain after another. The high air
hounds him into the sea, and the sea deposits him
in the dirt, which heaves him into the sunlight, and the sunlight
drives him back into the undertow of air. Each takes him
from the other, but none of them offers him shelter.
I am one of these, a vagrant, a refugee from gods.
Me. I believe in a drunken brawl.

7

They come among the animals as mountain cats
and among the broadleaf trees in the forms of laurels.

Blood and muscle: roughly equal
quantities of storm, earth,
fire, and the high clear air
spilling together into lagoons.

Bone: made in caverns out of
two parts earth and two parts luminous
hunger trapped with four parts starving fire.

The commentators say that Empedokles'
hunger is nothing but water.
And the commentators say
Empedokles' last formula was for

mind: made in volcanoes
out of cauterized eyes and vaporized
muscle, blood and bone.

VII PHEREKYDES

Pherekydes, in summary, thus: *In the beginning
were time, earth, and the god.
And the tissue of being*

*was woven by the god and given as a marriage gift
on the marriage of the underground and the god:
the embroidered surface of the world*

*thrown over the tree roots' wingspread, over the nakedness
of gods; and the thread-ends
swept out and forgotten.*

All things thereafter have been born
in the belly of the earth, in the seven
valleys, out of the seven inland streams.

Or a god put a veil on the ugly mud
and married it, and Pherekydes'
dust, when he was buried, sifted home.

There remains of the mind of Pherekydes:
the esker and the glacial milk,
the high spring runoff in the gorge,

and the waterfalls hammered out of cloud
against the mid cliff,
vanishing in the hungry Himalayan air.

VIII PYTHAGORAS

lemuribus vertebratis, ossibus inter tenebras

1

Remnants: the 39 rules, a sundial
untied like a shoelace, a theory of number
dismembered and scattered like dice. And the third-hand
chatter over the transmigration of souls.
And a story: Pythagoras wouldn't eat meat

and his legs buckled under him.
                              Rubble
of picked-over thought, shattered pediments, cracked
roof tiles laid up with mortar now gone in the rain.

Seabirds over the high grass,
nothing erect
except these pillars:
the mind of Pythagoras stands on two columns of words.

2

Not the calculus. Numbers. Integers
tethered into crystal structures: copper, antimony....
Integers driven like nails into inflexible void.

Dull-eyed disciples, centuries later, sitting
down to count the catalog,
mumbling over multipliers.

3

Unity is a substance, not a property. Light
is finite and motionless. Darkness
is the everlasting verb.

Strangeness is four-square.
Plurality curves,
the darkness is plural,
and only the left hand moves.

And the darkness ... this ... *these*
darknesses are everywhere.

The sundial's tooth is the token,
like a carpenter's rule. The sharpened
darkness is simply the index.
Light
does not move, but light is the tool.

4

The principle, therefore:
transparency.

Shaving the obsidian
to the clarity of the clean talon;
leaving no furrow or footprint or stripped stem,
no trace of rest between two intervals of motion;
the tongue to cast no shadow
on the word, the hand no shadow on the stone.

Darkness arcs over the head, said Pythagoras.
Forget the head. Paint portraits of the mind.
Darkness flows between closed fingers.
Draw me the god without the body. Only
the intangible tangency, sculpture like the plucked string,
speech on the model of inaudible singing.
The plane is tuned by tightening the line.

5

Octaves of silence
do not exist and do not echo. Intervals
of darkness disassemble
endlessly. *Do not drink*
the darkness, said Pythagoras.
The soul cannot become pure darkness.
Possibly. Possibly.

1

Bearing children is even more dangerous,
said Demokritos, than buying a mirror,
yet this wealth strangely easy to come by –
a bed and two books,
bread and fruit and a strong pair of shoes.
In spite of bad government there was good weather,
but after the heart the first thing
to sour is always the water.
The demon's summerhouse is the soul.

2

What is is no more than what isn't;
the is, no advance on the isn't. Is
is isn't with rhythm.
Touching and turning the isn't is is.
Not being is basic. As silence is,
isn't is – during, before, and after the sound.
Isn't is everywhere. In you. Outside.
Presence is absence keeping time.

3

That which splits off from the edgeless has edges.
It dries into light, it ignites into fire.
Fire and mind I believe to be
round, though knowledge is always
lopsided, like elm leaves.
Nose, eyes, ears, tongue
and fingers are fingers – all fingers
groping for imprints in the intermittent air.

4

Such giants we are, and so hardly
here, mere shapes in the dust, and our
deaf hands yelling so loud,
the diaphanous blood, the diaphanous
bone, and the truth so small as it crumbles it swims
in and out of the intestine,
floats through the ear's net, the eye's net,
the sieve of the palm.

5

A man must be ready for death
always, as sound must always be ready
for silence. There are of course contrary yearnings,
called information and music, but call it
laughter or call it beatitude,
a good joke is the most you can ask.

6

The uncountable rhythms uncountable
worlds – more in some places than others.
Motion, on closer inspection, appears
to be limited to reverberation and falling.
Never look down without turning.
Never live with your back to the mountains.
Never mend net with your back to the sea.

7

Thus the earth goes south each summer.
The mind moults in the north like a widgeon
and rises, hunting or grazing, in autumn,
riding the gale,
the stain of the voice like a handprint at intervals
in the unravelling rigging.

8

Incidentally you may notice,
said Demokritos,
the eagle has black bones.

X XENOPHANES

1

Earth is the ultimate substance.
What is, is made out of earth. We
who climb free of it,
milkthistles, mallards and men,
are made out of earth that is driven by water.

I have found chiton shells high
in the mountains, the finprints of fish
in the stonecutter's stone, and seen
boulders and trees dragged to sea
by the river. Water and earth
lurch, wrestle and twist in their purposeless
war, of which we
are a consequence, not an answer.

2

The earth gives birth to the sun
each morning, and washes herself in the water,
and slits the sun's throat every night
with a splintered stone, and washes
herself once again in the water.

Some days the sun, like a fattening
goose, crosses over in ignorant stupor.
Other days, watch: you will see him
shudder and twitch, like a rabbit
caught in the snare – but what
does it matter? One way
or the other, his death is the same.

We must learn to be thought
by the gods, not to think them.
Not to think gods have two eyes and ten fingers,
thirty-two teeth and two
asymmetrical footprints. Not to think
here in the unstoppered bowls
of our skulls we hold luminous
godbreath. The mush in our skulls
is compiled, like our toenails,
of rocksalt and silt, which is matted
like felt in the one case and swollen
like hope in the other.

What is, is earth. What dies
is earth driven by water.

3

The earth has one end. It is under
our feet. You may think
differently; I am convinced
there is no other.

from the Antigone *of Sophocles, a version*
in memory of Martin Heidegger, 1889–1977

Strangeness is frequent enough, but nothing
is ever as strange as a man is.
For instance,
out there,
riding the grey-maned water,
heavy weather on the southwest quarter,
jarred by the sea's thunder,
tacking through the bruise-blue waves.
Or he paws at the eldest of goddesses,
earth, as though she were made
out of gifts and forgiveness,
driving his plough in its circle year after year
with what used to be horses.

Birds' minds climb the air, yet he snares them,
and creatures of the field.
These
and the flocks
of the deep sea. He unfurls
his folded nets for their funeral shrouds.
Man the tactician.

So, as you see, by his sly
inventions he masters
his betters: the deep-throated
goats of the mountain,
and horses. His yokes ride the necks
of the tireless bulls who once haunted these hills.

And the sounds in his own throat
gather the breezes that rise in his mind.
He has learned how to sit on committees
and learned to build houses and barns
against blizzards and gales.
He manages all and yet manages
nothing. Nothing is closed
to the reach of his will,
and yet he has found no road out of hell.
His fate, we all know, is precisely
what he has never outwitted.

Wise, yes – or ingenious.
More knowledge than hope in his hand,
and evil comes out of it sometimes,
and sometimes he creeps toward nobility.
Warped on the earth's loom
and dyed in the thought of the gods,
a man should add beauty and strength to his city.
But he is no citizen whatsoever
if he is tied to the ugly by fear
or by greed or by love of disorder. May no one
who will not wonder what he is and what he does
suddenly arrive at my fireside.

inscription on gold foil, from a tomb in southern Italy,
perhaps 4th century BC

You will come to a well on the left side of hell's house.
A white cypress stands by it, luminous, pale.
Stay clear of this well at all cost. Don't drink from this well.
You will come to another, where cold water flows
from the marshes of memory. Sentinels stand there.
Say: *I am earth's and the starred sky's child, but the sky's*
blood runs in my veins; you can see this yourselves.
Thirst withers me. Hurry, give me
the cold water flowing from the lake of memory.
They will give you water from the sacred wellhead,
and you will be known . . . . heroes from then on.
. . . . going to die
. . . . this writing . . .
. . . . the darkness closing over.

☐ HACHADURA

Ahuachapán, El Salvador, 1969–74

a la memoria de los destruidos

I

There is a nothing like the razor
edge of air, another

like the tongued pebbles, syllables
of sea-wind and sea-colour and

another and another like the salt
hide drying inward, eating

in through the underbelly of the bone,
the grain

of the sea-eaten iron, and the open
lattice of the wave.

There is the nothing, moreover,
at which Eurytos never
quite arrives, tallying
the dust with the four-finger
abacus
unsheathed from the flesh of his hand.

Suppose, therefore, a certain
concretion of order,
unstable or at any rate in motion, but a certain
concretion of order inherent in one
of the innumerable
forms of such a number. Therefore:

darkness under the sunrise,
darkness in the hollow of the hand;

inside the spine the darkness, the darkness
simmering in the glands;

the rumpled blade of darkness that is
lodged in every fissure of the brain;

the membrane
of the darkness that is always

interposed
between two surfaces when they close.

II

The bird is the colour of gunmetal
in sunlight, but it is midnight;
the bird the colour of gunmetal
in sunlight is flying
under the moon.

There is a point at which
meridians are knotted
into nothing and a region
into which meridians fray and intertwine,
but not like mooring lines; they
fray like the leading and trailing edges
of wings, running from nothingness
to muscle and strung from the muscle back again.

Listen: the sounds are the sounds of meridians
trilling, meridians drawn to produce
the illusion of plectrum, tuning pegs and a frame,
or perhaps to produce Elijah's
audition: the hide
of the silence curing,
tanning,
tightening into the wind.

Or the sounds are the sounds of the air opening
up over the beak and closing over the vane,
opening over the unmoving cargo slung
between the spine and the talon,
slung between the wingbone and the brain.

III

It is for nothing, yes,
this manicuring, barbering, this
shaving of the blade.

Nothing: that is that the edge should come
to nothing as continuously
and cleanly and completely as it can.

And the instruction
is given, therefore,
to the archer, sharpening

the blood and straightening
the vein: the same instruction
that is given to the harper:

Tap.
Strum the muscle.
Breathe.

And come to nothing.

IV

Consider the magnetism of bone,
the blood-magnetic
fleshfield eddying in
and out of the marrow
under the blood-flux in the vein.

The apple is the palpable
aura and hysteresis
of the seed, the tissue is
a proof of the polarity and necessary
coldness of the bone.

V

In the high West there is everything
it is that the high West consists of,
mountains,
named animals and unnamed birds,

mountain water, mountain trees
and mosses, and the marrow of the air
inside its luminous blue bone.
And the light that lies just under darkness,
Artemis

grazing the ice
that is sea-rose under the sunset, and sea-green
and sea-deep under the snow's froth. Under
the still white water the sudden
fissure in the wave.

Measure from the surface,
measure from the light's edge
to the surface of the darkness, measure
from the light's edge to the sound.

VI

My Connecticut uncle stares into his manicured
thumbnail, thinking of his Riviera uncle's
smoked-glass monocle. A one-eyed sun-goggle,
halfway useful in the lethal roselight. Notice
nevertheless it seems the light drills
up the nerve backward, welling underneath
the retina and altering the eye's aim. Notice
that the coloured cores of the air lurch up
the ear, blue-gold and maroon against the blind drum.
Notice in addition the others at this intersection:
this one who is talking, this one who is standing
in the shoes of the man who is wearing them and sitting,
this one with, undeniably, a knife in his hand,
this one, this one saying nothing....

VII

Empedokles says the talon
is the crystallization
of the tendon, the nail is the wintered nerve.
Or the antler is the arrowhead
of the arrow threading the axeheads of the spine.

The Aristotelian then
wonders whether leather stands
in similar relation
to the muscle, and if sunlight might
be said to shed the darkness back of the stone.

VIII

The mules the angels ride come slowly down
the blazing passes, over the high scree
and the relict ice, through the lichen-spattered
boulders and the stunted timber. Slowly

but as noiselessly as is
proper to the progeny of sea-mares
and celestial asses. Down
through the gentian and the peppergrass, down
through the understory dark

between these trees, down through the recurved waves
and into unlightable water. The mules
the angels ride go to summer pasture
somewhere on the seafloor or still deeper.

IX

Chitin and calcareous accretions
no longer clothe me. Meat
has eaten the fossil;
the body is no longer able
to moult the bone.

Or as the field notes
show for August:
the squid has swallowed the quill; the animal
has successfully attempted
to incarcerate the cage.

X

The bud of light before the sunrise
mated with the dusk,
bore rock and jagged water,
mated with the water, bore
the tidal bore, the overfall, the spindrift and the mist.

The starlight seeded earth and mist and water,
germinating slime.
Slime ate into the rocksalt and the darkness,
the seacrust and the metamorphic stone, breeding
nail and nervecord, bone marrow, molar and

bones taking root in the darknesses
and darknesses
flowering out of the bone.
Gods and men and goddesses
and ghosts are grown out of this,

brothers of the bark and the heartwood and the thorn,
brothers of the gull and the staghorn coral,
brothers of the streptococcus,
the spirochete, the tiger, the albatross, the sea-spider,
cousins of lime and nitrogen and rain.

XI

In the blood's alluvium
there are alphabets: feldspars and ores,
silt jamming the mouths, and the sea's weight
or the white magmatic fire
is required to read the spoor:

the thumbprint on the air, the soul's print
beached on the foreshore under the slag,
the spine-tracks and excavations
of sea urchins
climbing the high crags.

XII

These, therefore, are the four
ages of man:
pitch-black, blood-colour, piss-colour, colourless.

After the season of iron the season
of concrete and tungsten alloy and plastic,
and after the season of concrete the season
of horn, born in the black October,

hooves and feathers hooves and feathers
shudder past the tusks
and navigate back between the horns.

□ THE STONECUTTER'S HORSES

Sepe de eo mecum cogitans de quo nemo nimis
pauci satis cogitant....

¶ Pavia, 4 April 1370:

Francesco Petrarca (1304–1374)

[Francesca], *his illegitimate daughter*

Franceschino da Brossano, *in law Petrarca's*
adopted son, but in actuality his son-in-law

I, Francesco, this April day…
death stirs like a bud in the sunlight, and Urban
has got off his French duff and re-entered Rome
and for three years running has invited me to Rome …
over the bright hills and down the Cassia,
back through Arezzo one more time …
my age sixty-five and my birthday approaching,
the muggers on the streets in broad daylight in Rome,
the hawks and the buzzards….
                                        Take this down.

No one has thought too deeply of death.
So few have left anything toward or against it.
Peculiar, since thinking of death can never be
wasted thinking, nor can it be come to
too quickly. A man carries his death with him
everywhere, waiting, but seldom thinking
of waiting. Death is uncommonly like the soul.

What I own other than that ought to fall
of its own weight and settle. But beggars and tycoons
and I are concerned with our possessions,
and a man with a reputation for truth
must have one also for precision.
                                        I leave
my soul to my saviour, my corpse to the earth.
And let it be done without any parades.
I don't care very much where I'm buried,
so it please God and whoever is digging.
Still, you will ask. You will badger me.
If I am dead you will badger each other.
But don't lug my bones through the public streets
in a box to be gabbled at and gawked at and followed.
Let it be done without any parades.

If I die here in Padova, bury me here
near the friend who is dead who invited me here.
If I die on my farm, you can use the chapel
I mean to build there, if I ever build it.
If not, try the village down the road.

If in Venezia, near the doorway.
If in Milano, next to the wall.
In Pavia, anywhere. Or if in Rome –
if in Rome, in the centre, of course, if there's room.
These are the places I think I might die in
in Italy.
    Or if I happen to be in Parma,
there is the cathedral, of which for some reason
I am the archdeacon. But I will avoid
going to Parma. It would scarcely be possible,
I suppose, in Parma, not to have a parade.

At any rate, put what flesh I have left
in a church. A Franciscan church if there is one.
I don't want it feeding a tree from which
rich people's children swipe apples.

Two hundred ducats go to the church in which
I am buried, with another hundred to be given
out in that parish to the poor, in small doses.
The money to the church, let it buy a piece of land
and the land be rented and the rental from the land
pay for an annual mass in my name.
I will be fitter company in that sanctuary
then, present in spirit and name only,
than this way, muttering to the blessed virgin
through my hemorrhoids and bad teeth. I should be glad
to be rid of this sagging carcass.
      Don't write that.

I have cleared no fields of their stones. I have built
no barns and no castles. I have built a name
out of other men's voices by banging my own
like a kitchen pan. My name to the Church
with the money it takes to have it embalmed.

Very few other things. My Giotto to the Duke.
Most men cannot fathom its beauty. Those
who know painting are stunned by it. The Duke
does not need another Giotto, but the Duke knows painting.

To Dondi, money for a plain ring to remind him
to read me.
            To Donato – what? I forgive him
the loan of whatever he owes me. And I
myself am in debt to della Seta. Pay
that, if I haven't paid it. And give him
my silver cup. Della Seta drinks
water. Damned metal ruins the wine.

To Boccaccio, I am unworthy to leave
anything, and have nothing worthy to leave.
Money then, for a coat to keep himself warm
when he works after dark, as he frequently does,
while the river wind stutters and bleats at his window,
and his hand-me-down cordwood fizzles and steams.

My lute to Tommaso. I hope he will play it
for God and himself and not to gain fame
for his playing.
            These are such trivial legacies.

Money to Pancaldo, but not for the card table.
Money to Zilio – at least his back salary.
Money to the other servants. Money to the cook.
Money to their heirs if they die before I do.

Give my Bible back to the Church.

                        And my horses …
my horses.

               Let a few of my friends, if they wish to,
draw lots for my horses. Horses
are horses. They cannot be given away.

The rest to my heir and executor, Brossano,
who knows he is to split it, and how he is to split it,
and the names I prefer not to put into this
instrument. Names of no other importance.
Care for them. Care for them here in this house
if you can. And don't sell off the land to get money
in any case. Selling the earth without cause
from the soul is simony, Brossano. Real-estate
hucksters are worse than funeral parades.
I have lived long enough in quite enough
cities, notwithstanding the gifts
of free lodging in some of them, long enough, Brossano,
to know the breath moves underfoot in the clay.
The stone quarried and cut and reset
in the earth is a lover's embrace, not an overlay.

The heart splits like a chinquapin pod,
spilling its angular seed on the ground.

Though we ride to Rome and back aboard animals,
nothing ever takes root on the move.
I have seen houses and fields bartered
like cargo on shipboard. But nothing takes root
without light in the eye and earth in the hand.

The land is our solitude and our silence.
A man should hoard what little silence
he is given and what little solitude he can get.

Just the one piece over the mountains
ought, I think, to be given away. Everything
I have ever done that has lasted began there.
And I think my heir will have no need to go there.

If Brossano die before I do,
look to della Seta. And for his part, let him
look into that cup. He will know my mind.

A man who can write as I can ought not
to talk of such things at such length. Keep this
back if you can. Let the gifts speak
for themselves if you can, small though they are.
But I don't like the thought of what little there is
spilling into the hands of lawyers through lawsuits.
The law is no ritual meant to be practised
in private by scavengers. Law is the celebration
of duty and the ceremony of vengeance. The Duke's
law has nothing to do with my death
or with horses.
    Done.
      Ask the notary to come over
precisely at noon. I will rewrite it
and have it to sign by the time he arrives.

☐ BONE FLUTE BREATHING

Поговорили и о литературе, но в приличных пределах.

They also talked of literature, but within decent limits.

Fyodor Dostoevsky
Бесы 2.4.3

These poems, these poems,
these poems, she said, are poems
with no love in them. These are the poems of a man
who would leave his wife and child because
they made noise in his study. These are the poems
of a man who would murder his mother to claim
the inheritance. These are the poems of a man
like Plato, she said, meaning something I did not
comprehend but which nevertheless
offended me. These are the poems of a man
who would rather sleep with himself than with women,
she said. These are the poems of a man
with eyes like a drawknife, hands like a pickpocket's
hands, woven of water and logic
and hunger, with no strand of love in them. These
poems are as heartless as birdsong, as unmeant
as elm leaves, which, if they love, love only
the wide blue sky and the air and the idea
of elm leaves. Self-love is an ending, she said,
and not a beginning. Love means love
of the thing sung, not of the song or the singing.
These poems, she said....
                    You are, he said,
beautiful.
          That is not love, she said rightly.

If a man see himself in a dream seeing his face in a mirror,
beware: it means another wife. – Papyrus Chester Beatty III,
British Museum (Thebes, 19th dynasty)

If a man should dream and should see himself dreaming
a dream, seeing himself in a mirror
seeing that the heart is oil riding
the blood like a lid toward which he is moving,
his bones like a boat and his gut strung up
for a sail in the wind of his breathing,

if this is his eye in the mirror seeing
his eye in the dream seeing himself
in a mirror seeing his eye seeing
himself in a dream in a mirror, his face
reflected in oil that ruffles from time
to time in the wind of his breathing,

the mirror will flow and the heart will set
like glass in the frame of his bones on the wall
of his breathing, his blood thin as paper and silver,
reflecting his face in his heart in a mirror
in a dream where he sees himself seeing
himself in a mirror seeing

that the bones will float and the heart will shatter,
his bones in his throat and his gut stretched tight
as a sail in the wind of his breathing, his blood
full of broken glass and his face like torn paper
seeing himself in the mirror of his heart
that scatters like oil in the mirror of his breathing.

It was not his face nor any
other face Narcissus saw
in the water. It was the absence there
of faces. It was the deep clear
of the blue pool he kept on coming
back to, and that kept on coming
back to him as he went to it, shipping
out over it, October after October
and every afternoon,
walking out of the land-locked summer,
out of the arms of his voice,
walking out of his words.

It was his eye, you may say,
that he saw there, or
the resonance of its colour.
Better yet, say it was what
he listened for – the low
whisper of light along the water, not
the racket among the stones.

Li Bó too. As we do – though
for the love of hearing
our voices, and for the fear of hearing
our speech in the voices of others come back
from the earth, we speak while we listen and look
down the long blue pools of air that come toward us and say
they make no sound, they have no
faces, they have one another's eyes.

for George Faludy

Before the black beak reappeared
like a grin from in back of a drained cup,
letting her drop,
she fed at the sideboard of his thighs,
the lank air tightening in the sunrise,
yes. But no, she put on no knowledge
with his power. And it was his power alone
that she saved of him for her daughter.
Not his knowledge.
No.
He was the one who put on knowledge.
He was the one who looked down out of heaven
with a dark croak, knowing more
than he had ever known before,
and knowing he knew it:

knowing the xylophone of her bones,
the lute of her back and the harp of her belly,
the flute of her throat,
woodwinds and drums of her muscles,
knowing the organ pipes of her veins;

knowing her as a man knows mountains he has hunted
naked and alone in –
knowing the fruits, the roots and the grasses,
the tastes of the streams
and the depths of the mosses,
knowing as he moves in the darkness he is also
resting at noon in the shade of her blood –
leaving behind him in the sheltered places
glyphs meaning mineral and moonlight and mind

and possession and memory,
leaving on the outcrops signs meaning mountain
and sunlight and lust and rest and forgetting.

Yes. And the beak that opened to croak
of his knowing that morning creaked like a rehung
door and said nothing, felt nothing. The past
is past. What is known is as lean
as the day's edge and runs
one direction. The truth floats
down, out of fuel,
indigestible, like a feather. The lady
herself, though – whether
or not she was truth or untruth, or both, or was neither –
she dropped through the air like a looped rope,
a necklace of meaning, remembering
everything forward and backward –
the middle, the end, the beginning –
and lit like a fishing skiff gliding aground.

That evening, of course, while her husband, to whom
she told nothing, strode like the king
of Lakonia through the orchestra
pit of her body, touching
this key and that string in his passing,
she lay like so much
green kindling,
fouled tackle and horse harness under his hands
and said nothing, felt
nothing, but only
lay thinking
not flutes, lutes and xylophones,
no: thinking soldiers
and soldiers and soldiers and soldiers
and daughters,
the rustle of knives in his motionless wings.

Simple enough. At the sound of him singing
their names, rocks, trees, middle-aged
women and most of the rest of creation
shot straight for his head and collided.

Since then it has been
the custom with musical
children
to put out the eyes.

Sailors and the hill people
buried what they could find of him.
Adolescents, potential
suicides and the wounded

attempted the names.
Safe in each case, as it happened –
like all the others – in their own
pronunciations.

Afterward too, the explainers
moved through the towns with their versions
and justifications.
They said, for example, the song

was brought on by a woman.
One of them said that the red-headed
woman who loved him had left
and was dead when he found her.

Another insisted he'd killed her. A third
told a long and haphazard story
in which she had gone on a pilgrimage
down the valley and met, unexpectedly

but quite simply, a better man,
with a liking for conversation
and chess, and a milder
face and a foreign name.

They said that the death had nothing to do
with shaped light or the sheer
edges of the air. They said he had sung
the earth wide open and walked in,

either to bury her or to retrieve her,
and almost succeeded. They said when he slipped
he was on the way up; he ought to have known
not to look down.

Or they said he died like a midge,
of his own luminescence,
or it was darkness and light that he named
and they came together and killed him.

Still in the hills they tell simpler stories.
They say his voice shone
like a blue stone. Some of them say
it was air he drank when he was thirsty,

water he breathed. It may have been only
his hands, some of them say,
that gave way, crushed
when the words closed over him;

and for days his voice
could be seen overhead, next to the sun,
his name tasted in the wellwater,
wind out of season heard in the young grain.

All light since
has bent through his silence.

Since then it has been
the custom with musical
children
to put out the eyes.

POEM WITHOUT VOICES

The light that blooms in your body
blooms in my hands. Around us the ground
is strewn with its petals.

I have seen on a street in Guadalajara
wind set the petals of a jacaranda
down on the ground surrounding a pine.

Love, this is evergreen; let it be.
You will see, they fall also. Listen
again: the silences

ripen
deep in the sullen beaks
of the intricate wooden flowers.

They say that a woman with steel-gray
eyes has lived for a thousand years
in these mountains. They say that the music
you almost hear in the level blue light
of morning and evening is music she played
in these mountains many years ago
on a flute she'd cut from the cannon bone
of a mule deer buck she'd tracked and wrestled
to the ground.
              They say that at the first few notes
she played, her sisters started giggling, because,
instead of listening, they were watching
the change that came over her face.
She stalked off in anger, and for years thereafter
only in darkness did anyone ever hear
the flute. Day after day
it lay silent on the mountain,
half hidden under a whitebark pine.
No one else was permitted to touch it,
much less to watch her while she played.

But a man came by one day from another
country, they say, who had never heard either
the flute or the story, and he found the flute
on the ground, under the pine tree, where it lay.
As soon as he put it to his lips, it played.
It breathed her music when he breathed,
and his hands began to find new
tunes between the tunes it played.

Angry once again at this intrusion,
the woman who lives in these mountains
complained about the stranger to her brother,
who lived on the other side of the world.

That very afternoon, her brother built
an elk's skull and antlers and a mountain cat's
intestines into a guitar, and as
he walked here, he taught himself to play.

Coming over the hills that way,
without a name, one stranger to another,
he challenged the stranger with the flute to a musical
duel to be judged by the woman who lives
in these mountains.
                        It may be the stranger, as many people say,
was simply unwary. It may be
the sun slivered his eyes that day
in such a way that he could see only
one choice. In any case, everyone
says that he consented to the contest.

They played night and day, and the stranger,
while he listened, watched the eyes,
and when they wandered, watched the lips
of the woman who lives in these mountains.
Sister, said the eyes: *sister of the other
who is playing the guitar.* But the lips said, *Music
of the breath, music of the bone.* And the breath
of the woman, whether she willed it to or no,
kept moving in the flute whenever the stranger
played. After seven nights and days,
everyone knew the stranger was the winner.

That was when the man with the guitar said,
*Stranger, can you sing? Stranger, can you sing us
a song along with the music you play?
Listen,* said the man with the guitar,
and I will show you what I mean.
And while the woman and the stranger watched
and listened, the man with the guitar stared
hard into the air, and his hands like water spiders

flickered over the guitar, and a song slid
out between his teeth and flowed
through the music he played.

The stranger in his turn stared
hard into the air and far into the eyes
of the woman who lives in these mountains.
And the eyes stared back, and the eyes said, *These
are the eyes of the sister of the other,* and the stranger
played and the stranger played, and no word
came. He stared long at her lips,
and the lips said, *Bone.* The lips said,
Wordless breath in the bone. And breathe
as he would, he could not
sing through the music he played.

So it was that the woman with the steel-gray
eyes, gazing into the whitebark
pine behind both of them, quietly declared
the man with the guitar to be the winner.

She reached for the flute,
but her brother stepped in front of her.
He picked up the flute and the guitar
and smacked them one against the other and against
the rocks until both of them shattered.

Then, taking the stranger by the throat,
he threw him flat against the ground.
And taking a splinter from the flute,
and moving swiftly, like a crouching
dancer, he peeled the living flesh
away from the stranger's feet and hands.
He peeled his face and hips and ribs
and neatly filleted each of his limbs.

One by one he extracted the stranger's
bones, and one by one he replaced them
with the splinters of the deerbone flute
and the shattered skull and antlers
that had been his own guitar.

He stitched the splinters into the stranger's
fingers, into his head and chest
and limbs with the mountain cat's intestines,
and set him on his feet, and propped the last splinter
of the bone flute upright in his hand,
and walked off, stopping to scrub
his own hands in a shrinking bank
of spring snow, never uttering a sound.

The stranger stood there motionless
for years – but they say that the music you almost
hear in the level blue light of morning
and evening, now, is the sound of the stranger
moving, walking back toward his own country,
one step at a time.

☐ TZUHALEM'S MOUNTAIN

A Sonata in Three Movements

I   PARABLE OF THE THREE ROCKS

I have seen in the mountains a man pluck
birdsnest lichen from the limb of an alpine
fir, where it hung in the wind like sea-green
goat hair; I have seen him gather three
white stones, as sharp and clear as milkteeth.

I have seen him lay these cracked
pieces of rock into the deep
cup of the nest like a creature
half hunter, half long-legged bird,

and seen him carry them away: three
razor-sharp stones: two
to stand for two lovers
and a third to stand for the world.

I have seen three razor-edged, milk-white
stones in a nest of sea-green lichen
on a table and heard them explained to inquisitive
visitors as the teeth of deepwater fishes
or the eggs of carnivorous birds.

II   PARABLE OF THE HARPS

In the drum of the heart
are the hoofbeats of horses – the horse
of the muscles, the horse of the bones.

In the flutes of the bones are the voices
of fishes – the fish of the belly,
the fish of the fingers and limbs.

In the streams of the limbs
we are swimming with fishes
and fording with lathering horses.

Love, in this bed full of horses
and fishes, I bring to the resonant gourds
of your breasts the harps of my hands.

III   PARABLE OF THE YEW TREES

In this bed full of horses
and fishes, carnivorous birds
are leading us down into oceans
and up into mountains. My love,
in this bed full of fishes and horses,
carnivorous birds are screaming
their names and repeating their stories,
though no one can hear them.

They say we are falling like foraging
ospreys, they say we are climbing
like laddering salmon up out of the sea,
we are climbing like horses
up into the mountains filled with the sounds
of carnivorous birds. They say
we are carnivorous birds, climbing
up out of the mountains, climbing the air.

They say when we reach there
in the salt mirrors of your eyes
I will see only birds, and you
on the walls of my eyes only fishes.
They say in this bed full of fishes
and birds, all the men you have known
will ride through your face and fall
from their horses, drowning in sunlight and ashes,

the ospreys will dive and the salmon will climb
from the sea and the yew trees will lend us their voices,
though nothing we say with them then
will reach through these distances.

IV BODY, SPEECH AND MIND

In the high passes the stones turn,
tuning the air. They are silent
who live there. As the cat
kills at the throat and then opens
the belly, those who can speak
lurk back toward the valley,
into the alder over the river,
where the air is played.

This is tuning and playing, love,
this is both, this is knowing and saying,
this is the dark heart of the bone
breathing like pine trees, this
is the heart like a claw in the ground.

This is the sound of the body
singing, the voice in its place,
under cliffs, by the bloodstream,
holding the skull in its outstretched
arms like an overturned bowl,
and singing, and singing
the song they dream near the rocks
in the difficult air.

V PARABLE OF THE STREAM

Love, he has seen them
before, he has known
they were there,
scattered and gleaming.
Now in the clear
stream of your flesh
he is panning for bones.

VI PARABLE OF THE THINKER

Love, in the bright
mirrors of your eyes
in the dark I have seen him
again: I have seen there
the great, angular
bird who feeds in the mountains
on the thinker's pain.

VII PARABLE OF THE TWO BIRDS

I have seen in the mountains a shape
like two birds with three wings
between them and seen them
swooping, seizing the same fish

from the stream and hovering
there until the shared wing
opened. I have seen the dark bone glide
like a knife blade out of the feathers.

In the shadow of their wings I have seen then
the same thing happen to the fish:

the one bird suddenly clutching fins and flesh,
the other with the head and skeleton.

Love, the bird with the feathers took the flesh
of the fish and floated toward the ocean.
The bird with the bone wing rose
toward the peaks, and in his talons hung the skeleton.

Love, I have felt the world part in our hands.

§

VIII FIRST LIGHT

Hawk and owl in the dead
red alder: daybird and nightbird asleep in the tree
while the spilled light builds in the snowchutes
high on the mountain.

Unopened, like roses,
the milk-smooth, identical faces
of those I have loved for the eloquence
of their pain.

IX QUESTIONS FOR THE OLD WOMAN

From the hills of your breasts to the ruined wells
of your eyes is how many miles, old woman?
And how many days to the outwash fans
and gravelled channels of your thighs?

Old woman, what do we know but the swollen
thumb of the tongue against the cranium?
What do we know but the bloodshot
knuckles of the eyes,

the sting of the light in the tightening
fist, the ache of the darkness caked
in the hand? What do we know but the innocent
songs of the lungs in their cage never mating?

What do we know but the dry rasp
of a banjo pick against paper, the whisper
of blood against wood in the stunted trunk
of a tree, uprooted and running?

Old woman, the hungry
ghosts as they gather
lick dry lips and gibber
against your thighs.
What will you
say as you chase them
away? You can neither
ignore them nor feed them.
Your fingers are chanting
already to chase them
away, and what
will you say? They are singing
with swollen tongues,
the dead are dying
of thirst, the dead
are dying of thirst,
with swollen tongues
in their broken lips
they are singing. They say
if I play you will sing me
a song of the flesh,
old woman, the wisdom
of fish who swim up
from the ocean, the wisdom
of birds who return
to their tundra
year after year
down the winding canyons
of the air, the immense
wisdom, old woman,
of trees who remain
in their places, embracing
the earth, the wisdom
in summer of hummingbirds,
mouth to mouth

in the air with the open-mouthed
flowers, the ripe
sisters surrounded
by rubbernecked brothers,
old woman, the wisdom
of men who emerge
from the sea and descend
through the mouths of the mountain.
Old woman, they say
you will sing if I play
on the unstrung lute
of your back, on the cracked
piano built
of your bones, on the wrinkled
guitar in the threadbare
case of your body.
Old woman, the banjo
hangs like an arrowless
bow in your belly,
but they say if I can play it
you will sing. They say
you will sing me
the words of the song.

XI   SONG OF TZUHALEM

Belly and back
beak of the bird
claw of the cat
plucking the taut

muscle and gut
beak of the bird
belly and back
claw of the cat

plucking the taut
muscle and gut
claw of the cat
belly and back

beak of the bird
plucking the taut
muscle and gut
belly and back

beak of the bird
claw of the cat
plucking the taut
muscle and gut

belly and back
beak of the bird
beak of the bird
claw of the cat

XII   HIC AMOR, HAEC PATRIA

Old woman, a man
comes into the mountains
alone in high summer
because he is eaten.
His body is eaten
by darkness in winter,
his mind is eaten
in spring by the deepening
pulse of his hunger.
The bees know his blood
on the hillside in summer
as bright as red heather.
The birds know his blood

on the mountain in autumn
as black as empetrum.

Old woman, a man
comes into the mountains
to make himself whole.
Why is it the knife
of love redivides us?
Why is it a man
cannot heal the wounds
in a woman by bringing
her also up into
these mountains?

Old woman, old woman,
her body like water,
her flesh like a fish,
the wind in the air
underlying her name.

All knowledge is carnal.
Knowledge is meat,
knowledge is muscle.
Old woman, old woman,
what is this hunger
grown hard as a bone?

XIII   LONICERA INVOLUCRATA

Mouth to mouth, our faces
closing one another's faces,
the lids of our skulls
closing one another's eyes.

And the ghosts of the butterscotch eyes
of Tzuhalem in pairs in the twilight

like twinberry flowers.
Ghosts of his women
probe for their nectar like needle-beaked birds.

The waxwing sits
in the willow tree, waiting.

In the wilted light,
the beaten blue metal of the sea.

XIV   LAST LIGHT

Herons croak from the broken hemlocks.
Herons glide beneath Tzuhalem's
mountain. The heart, like a bat going out
after moths in the shadows, unfolds and floats, singing

to rocks, trees and its prey, its shrill
but inaudible syllables pulsing and quickening,
eats, and retreats once again to the stench
of its cave, strung up by one foot, with the other foot

bathing.

§

XV PARABLE OF THE MOON

In the cave of the moon
thirteen women are moving.
At new moon a man
with three shoulders will rise
and move with them, his three-shouldered
dancing joined to their dancing
in front of the fire.

XVI PARABLE OF THE TRUTH

Love, I love, I
do not love, no
it is true, I do not
love, but I love you
anyway, as well
as I am able
in these difficult
conditions. What
can a man come back
to say, who does not
know the word
hello, who never said
goodbye, and also
does not know
if he has ever reached
or left his destination?

XVII PARABLE OF THE VOICES

Behind the heart
is a deaf musician
beating a broken

drum. He is watching
the animals leap
through the hoops of our voices.

The air is another
earth full of burrows
the animals enter
and leave through the doors
of our voices. Down through our voices
the waterbirds dive.

XVIII HIS DREAM

In his hands is a face
full of fossils and pebbles.
A mask. It comes out of
the lake where a man
who is dying is trying
to drown and keeps failing.

The faces afloat
on the water are never
his own. When they shatter
he holds them together.

They show him the mask.
He goes with them, and when
he returns, all the faces
he sees are like faces
in water. They shatter.
He holds them together.

He calls to his sister
to help him. She baits
a fishline with feathers
and casts, and the faces

come up from the water
and shatter. Out of
the jagged pieces
of faces, she gathers
the mask. When he wears it
his hands twitch like rattles.

XIX   PARABLE OF THE LAKE'S EDGE

Old woman, a man
must stand on his shadow
to fish from the shore
of the lake of the daylight.
Morning and evening
his shadow is moving.
Morning after morning
a man must rename
the sun without breathing.
Morning after morning
a man standing still
as a stick at the lake's edge
must gather the dance
in his hands without moving.

XX   PARABLE OF THE INDESTRUCTIBLE

Where is it now, the golden bough
I carried through her body?
Where is the taste of sweet water
torn from our mouths? And why is it

the birds who can sing never enter
the water or hunt from the mountain?
Listen: the bleat of the widgeon,
the moan of the loon and the croak of the heron,

the hawks howling like wolves and the sea eagles
neighing like horses, the gibber of gulls,
and the small owl barking in daylight:
like bones in their throats their own

indestructible questions.

XXI   PARABLE OF THE SUN

Bright fish in the shallows
breaking their guts to come home to these gravels,
their bowels chewed by the unborn,
their backs by the eagles.

The man in the sun, savaged
by cats, drags his cloak through the waters
and limps up the mountain,
his footprints in tatters.

☐   THE BOOK OF SILENCES

一切時中但有語言道斷即是自心

I SHORT UPANISHAD

Give us places, said the gods.
She made a cow, a horse, a goose, a human being.
Wait, said the gods, we asked for places.

These are places, he replied.
The palm of the hand is a place.
So is the mouth; so is the eye; so is the mind.

Hunger and thirst said,
Where is our place?
She answered, Sit beside the gods.

II PARŚVANATHA

What is whole has no face. What
is apart from the whole has no body.

Yet somehow it is, and it is
manysided. Somehow it isn't
and is manysided. Somehow
it is manysided and isn't
and is. It cannot be touched
by the mind or by language, but somehow,
in spite of our thinking and talking,
it is, and in spite of our thinking
and talking, it isn't. Beyond
all our thinking and talking,
it isn't and is. This
is a map of our knowing. Own
nothing. Like breath in your lungs,

the truth passes through you.
Where space, motion and rest
come together is being. Where being
is tainted by death, you find
matter. Like water through cloth,
the unbroken plasma of action
drains through your bones.
What you are will be spelled by whatever
lies trapped in your hand.

On the fenceposts, the weathering heads of your brothers
are thinking of nothing. And speechless. And singing.

III   NAGARJUNA

What is is swollen like a ripe
fruit, hollow like a cave.
What you touch, hear, taste, see, smell
is the inner perfection of vision.

What reaches into our eyes and our ears
is what is, and that is the wordless, inaudible
song and the brooding, unmusical
speech of the world.

This too
is just one
more opinion
to move through.

What is is what lies
out of sight, thought and talking.
Open them. Open the three
fists clinging to the world.

Open this too.
All positions
are prisons.
No truth is true.

No instruction is certain, no knowledge complete.
If I speak for the serpent, the serpent
may speak for the bird. My position
is that I have no position.

This too.
All fictions
are true,
all intentions,

positions,
and all dispositions
are prisons;
this too.

What is has no essence.
What is is interdependent and empty.
What is is unsingle, undouble, unplural, unborn,
unenduring, unbearing, undying;

what is has no past and no future, no shape
and no nature, no being, no having been, going
to be or becoming, no wholeness and no
incompleteness, no fingers....

This too.
This too
is just one
more opinion.

Outside the perfection of light there is no
total darkness. What causes what is is the hunger
to be and keep being. What is is on loan
from what isn't and is its reflection.

*What is is on loan from what isn't and is
its disguise.* There is no rock bottom.
No centre, no sides, no top and no bottom.
This too.

There are no literal statements.
There is no unmetaphorical language.
This too.
Emptiness also is empty.

Nothing is not nothing. Nothing
is, and *is* is nothing. All that is
is nothing, yet there is
no nothing there that we can cling to.

*We are also then
the nothing,*
and the nothing
is the hunger,

*and the hunger
is the question*
and the answer:
be pure wonder.

I cut off my eyelids,
he cut off his arm.
He could not hold the cleaver
to cut off the other.

He could have kept both
had he noticed this sooner.
The scars of our errors
are taken for signs.

There is no other side
to this wall, though the road
is so wide it leads through.
It leads through. That is all.

V SENGZHAO

The thought of the gods is dark water. The gods
have their destinies too as they move through the world.
Our speech does not reach them. As for our speechlessness,
what shall we say? And to whom shall we say it?
What is is not easy and graceful to speak of.
My teacher, a foreigner, lame in the tongue
like a caged raven, knew this.
I, however, was born here. Forgive me,
that sometimes I sink into elegant phrase.

The gods' minds and their mindprints are one
and the same. With us it is different. Our footprints
fall off as we walk through the world. Our brilliant
assertions tack like October leaves

through the air before mouldering. Yes and no
are at home in each other, not elsewhere. What is
and who knows of its presence are one and the same.

The feet are the link
between earth and the body. Begin there.
The lungs are the link between body and air.
The hands, these uprooted feet, are the means
of our shaping and grasping. Clasp them.
The eyes are the hands of the head;
its feet are the ears.

We are all of us here in the hidden
house of the unnamed. You
who insist we must visit
and name it have ceased to be there.

VI   YONGJIA XUANJUE

Not a river, a road. What flows without flowing.
The sentence we read and reread
with our feet, not the pages we write
and rewrite and rewrite with our hands.

What is is wherever the living
are walking. It limps through the earth,
swims through the water, flies through the air,
and it runs the full distance without ever moving.

What is is wherever the living
are walking. Not where the dead have planted
their flags. Where the living are walking, the dead,
the unborn and the newborn are comfortably riding.

Your hand cannot hold it; your mind
cannot leave it behind. When you chase it,
it runs. When you walk, it comes toward you.
Wherever you stand, it sprouts all around.

How many self-portraits and portraits emerge
from the face every day, and how many
return? If you stay, you have left; if you come,
you are staying. This much is the same for all time.

Not a river, a road. Yet Mr Old
and Mr Serious, Mr Nostril and Anonymous
are walking by the stream, which speaks with each one
of their uninterchangeable voices.

Reader, great grandmother, grandfather, friend,
please come here this minute and speak to me,
as the trees do, as the wind does, if you also
have something, as they do, to say.

VII SARAHA

What is
is what isn't. What isn't
is water. The mind is a deer.
In the lakes of its eyes,
the deer and the water
must drink one another.
There are no others,
and there are no selves.
What the water sees
is – and is not what you think
you have seen in the water.

There is no something, no nothing,
but neither. No is
and no isn't, but neither. Now,
don't defile the thought
by sitting there thinking.
No difference exists
between body and mind, language
and mind, language and body.
What is, is not. You must love
and let loose of the world.

I used to write poems,
and like yours, they were made
out of words, which is why
they said nothing.
My friend, there is only one word
that I know now, and I have somehow
forgotten its name.

VIII   SARAHA'S EXERCISE FOR BEGINNERS

What is the brain but the back of the face?
Climb down from the elephant
of the mind you are riding, climb down
and leave it to drink
or to drown in the river.

What stirs in the heart
comes to rest in the heart
like dust in a cave.

Thought is thought, and not
anything more. Seeing is seeing.
What is is what is. These three together

are what they are, and their total is one,
which is what there is and is equal
to zero. A is not A; one is not one;
this too is the rule.

Only insofar as one is
speechless can one really
think with words.

IX BAIZHANG HUAIHAI

The mind appears to be
because of what the mind
appears to think of.
Nothing is external. Only

knowing is external. Only
knowing is beyond the reach
of knowing. Pure unbeing
is a seamless understanding of the world.

When it is known that there is
no such thing as knowing,
thought that no such thing as thinking
is, then thinking comes to pass.

In all of what is, there is
nothing quite lifeless.
No one who falls can rise
without help from the ground.

The ground is external.
What is is what you cannot
carry with you and what can't
be left behind.

X HAN SHAN

Friends, the mind, or at any rate
my mind at this moment, is much
like the moon. It is swollen
with light, it is dry and in motion.

Its taste and its smell, its feel
in the skull, are those of the moon
over the steep hills and the bottomless
pools of deep autumn.

Friends, what is is much like the pool.
What is not is not unlike the air,
and what neither is nor is not neither is
nor is not like or unlike the hills.

This being so, there is no
comparison, is no description, assertion,
negation. I tell you conclusively,
there can be no conclusions.

I am leaving now. Please,
no applause. Those who know how to live
will leave with me
in different directions.

1

Come in. Have some tea.
There is water in the pot,
and there is fire in the stove.

But everything I have to say is written
on the thin slips of darkness
in the closed book: the black leaves

you don't see when you open it – though
each one slips into its place again
as soon as you turn the page.

2

When the wind speaks, wind listens.
When stones speak, stones
hear what they say.

Going over the old bridge,
if you see yourself in the stream, what
message can you give to your reflection?

1

Take no shit, said Línjì.
Behead the Buddhas. Cow the pig of the world.

Take hold of it, use it, but do not
give it a name: this is the ultimate principle.

Sleep, eat, pee:
this is the essence of the way.

Build a boat in the mountains,
cut steps in the sea,

but no speculation, no fortification, no bridges,
burned or unburned.

There is nothing to do. The answer
is perched on your lips like a bird.

If it nests in your mouth, how will you speak?
How will you weave if it nests in your hands?

Singing and dancing! These are the signs
of the silent and still.

Is? No. Isn't? No. Is and isn't? Neither is nor isn't?
None of these. None of these and more.

What you see in the eyes of the deer as it wheels
and flees is not terror but horror.

Only a man with no hands
can reorder the world.

2

And so,
to begin with, leave home –
if something has made you imagine
you have one. Examine your face

in the mirror of the air,
and sit down with the man
who laughs when you ask him
his name, occupation, address.

Dying is one more simple thing everyone does,
like scratching the ear and undressing.

Thought and not thinking
are one. Is and isn't
are one. Sword, swordsman, stroke
and not striking are one. One and not one

are one. One is not two. One is also
not one. This arithmetic
lives in the flowering
heart of the world.

XIII DONGSHAN LIANGJIE

There is one tree growing
in the worked earth, one bird flying.
The stone woman rises to dance
when the wooden man sings.

The bird and the tree have no hands. With their mouths
they eat; with their feet they stay put;
with their arms they trace the original
shapes of the mountains.

Go up and look down. If the spirits
can find you to bring you
your dinner, your mind is unclear
and your meditation imperfect.

Saints and great teachers do not
know reality. Mountain cats, bristlecone
pines, wild buffalo do.
Though you are not it, it is certainly you.

You may only agree if you disagree
equally. Those who agree with their brothers
completely have stolen their shoes
when invited to mend them.

A sky full of migrating birds
is a mind, not a text to be studied
for seconds or centuries. One plus one
plus one equals one equals many.

One minus one equals equally many. The geese
cross and are gone. Below them the stones
have learned how to dance and the trees
how to fly without leaving their places.

The sages have learned how to breathe
through their ears, how to eat with their eyes.
Time and again they forget
to open and close them.

Stones and trees are my teachers, but
there are others. The truth of the world
sparkles in slopbuckets, toilet bowls, turds,
and in festering sores.

Are your eyes plugged up with light,
your ears plugged up with music
and your nose with sweet spring air?
Everything that has ever existed is medicine.

Bright emptiness burns in the doorway.
In the cupboard it fills up the dishes and bowls.
The flames in the stove are reciting the law.
Past, present and future have come here to listen.

XV   FAYAN WENYI

Where are you going? he said,
and I said, I don't know. Not knowing
is close, he said. Soon after that,
I decided to stay in one place for a while.

The local tradition is this:
that waking and dreaming, arriving and leaving,
are flower and stem. That we are where we are,
eating the answer each day, and excreting the question:

giving back shit, which the flowers and fireflies
eat, or hiding the shit, or feeding
the shit to our friends and our children,
and giving back nothing.

The whole is the truth, which is here
just as we are, tying its shoe, with its coat on one shoulder.
The truth, like the rest of us, dies and is born
and goes on with the business of living.

What shall I do with the night and the day,
with this life and this death? Every step, every
breath rolls like an egg
to the edge of this question.

XVI   XUEDOU ZHONGXIAN

There is no person. There are no words.
There is this moment, silent and speaking.
What seem to be beings are facets of time
permitted to dance in the light or to listen.

All eyes shine toward
one another; all eyes shine away.
What will your first words be, now that your last
have already been spoken?

Self-expression is easy. Expressing what is
is a little more difficult.
Orioles sing. The kingfisher chortles
and falls like an axe through a hole in the rain.

If you like, we could visit the one with the answers.
Each step is exactly halfway to her home.
The knife you must take has no tang and no handle,
the hammer no socket and shaft.

Standing invisibly in the hills,
walking inaudibly on the seafloor,
the one you can talk to will use
neither silence nor speech to reply.

There is only one way. It goes every direction.
The seventy joints of the body are knotholes
through which the turtles peer out of the river,
through which the sea-turtles enter the sea.

The circle is square,
and its corners are everywhere.
Carry your nostrils out into the woods with you,
one in each hand.

XVII DANXIA ZICHUN

The whole earth closes
like a fist and touches,
once, the rimless drum,

and opens
slowly as a rose
while no one listens.

The skull on the hill
wakes from its dream
before morning.

Impeccably dressed
though it is
in moonlight and moss,

and well fed, and well
rested, it gives
not a thought to returning.

XVIII DAHUI ZONGGAO

The truth is not for contemplation.
Just to know the odours of the truth
you must inhale the whole world
and be inhaled by the world in your turn.

To learn the flavours and the textures of the truth,
you must bite, chew and swallow the whole world –
every answer, every question – and be bitten,
chewed and swallowed in your turn.

The truth is not for contemplation.
I have burned my teacher's books.
I have burned my teacher's books,
and now, together, we will read them.

XIX TIANTONG RUJING

The names of my parents and teachers
are silences, zeroes. I learned what I know
by not knowing. I passed my exams
and presented my thesis by cleaning latrines.

134

A man raising his voice to silence an echo
has nothing to say but has not learned to say it.
Creation is set to begin at this moment.
The time before anything was is right now.

Shedding body and mind is like lifting your foot.
Setting it down is like shedding the shedding.
The bridge you are guarding crosses the stream
as fast as it can. The bridge I am walking
is flowing. Its footings are snowmelt and rain.

XX DOGEN

1

The mind is old snow, new snow, brooding rain.
The mind is lichen crust and stone.
Pebbles and sticks are the fountains of wisdom.

Go into the hills and remain there forever.
Wise as a snowflake that lives
for ten minutes, wise as a stone

that is young at three million years,
let the trees make your gestures,
the gutters your prayers.

Pass the note of yourself to the river
to read to the hills. Let the wind and the leaves
speak your thoughts in their language.

Many or few: any number will do. This
is the world, and the world is one – either one –
and neither and both of your eyes.

And your face is its face. And the eyes in your face
are the eyes you have seen,
seeing you, in the faces of others.

2

One drop of blood, one drop
of falling rain contains
the final truth, the temporary
lie, the day, the night,
the earth, the sky,
the light, the dark, the still
unfurling world.

3

Under the sunrise the mountains
are walking on water.
This is the skin.
The mountains are dancing.
They are walking on their toes
on all the water in the world.
This is the blood.
And all the water in the world –
oceans, raindrops, runoff dipped
in cupped hands, moistened lips and tears –
is holding up the mountains.
This is the ligament. This is the bone.

The bones are flowing water.
There is marrow in the bone.
Never judge by just one word.
Never judge by just one world.
In the marrow is the blood.
If the mountains stop walking, the world
will stop being born.

4

Everything that is is the foundation of the mind.
Everything that is is root and stem
and fruit and flower,
head and tail, back and belly, belly and bum.

Everything that is is every
time that ever was
or is or will be and is
passing through the heart between your hands.

5

There is no pigment in the paint.
There are no bristles in the brush.
There is no hand.

There is no lid or lens
or retina in the eye.
And all the same,

the painting you have come to see
can see the forms and colours
that you are, which are

the world's forms and colours
in your size. The silence
you have come to see

can see you breathe; the breath you breathe
can hear the painted man in whom
this painted voice is speaking.

6

Everyone goes to the mountains,
yet no one is there.
That is only to say
that we are who we are
and mountains are mountains.
The mountains are coming to us,
and no one is here.

The mountains are flowing,
the water is still,
Dōgen is sitting.
His mind is a lake looking upward,
a sky looking down.

Inside the dead man's breath, the living breathe.
Inside the living woman's pain,
the dead, pretending to be soldiers,
hunt for sons and enemies and joy.
The hungry ghosts, disguised as living beings,
are sucking their own bones.

The hungry ghosts grow younger,
crawling backward through the womb.
They swarm like angry hornets through the loins.
Dancing, broken
arm in arm with mountains,
is not a children's game.

XXI JAKUSHITSU

Wind through the warp
of the waterfall, talking.
Moon above the hill across the harbour,
climbing and gleaming.

When I am dead and my bones lie
mindlessly in the dirt,
they will be
as transparent as ever.

XXII BANKEI

Light leaks from the mind like
tears from the eye,
blood from the body.

It flows from what-is like
sap from the tree. That is the only
reliable language.

What is is unborn.
Nevertheless,
it is already bearing.

The source of what was
is what is, and the source of what is
must be what will be.

What is is unborn.
What is born is a gesture
toward or away.

At the ends of the nerves,
what will be is breeding.
Being is bearing.

In bones and in river silt,
chromosomes, leaf-shapes,
in starlight and synapse and stone,

what no longer exists
is just shaving its face
and choosing its clothes.

What is is not yet born
and never will be,
yet these very words,

these very words
are listening
for all you have to say.

☐ LYELL ISLAND VARIATIONS

Hlqiiya Lnagaai, Haida Gwaii

… es sind / noch Lieder zu singen jenseits / der Menschen
        – Paul Celan

In the threadbare
air, through the tattered
weave of leaves,
the blue light cools
into ash-black shadow.

Tree: the high
thought roots itself
in the luminous clay
of the caught light's closeness
to audibility.

So we know that again
today, there are songs
still to be sung. They
exist. Just on the other
side of mankind.

… et la terre mauvaise dans le champ de son cœur
          – René Char

Once upon a time there was a man
who never hungered anymore,
or so I heard – he had devoured so many legacies,
bitten off anything, eaten through anyone who came near –

who one day found
that his table was cleared,
his bed emptied, his children renamed,
and the soil gone sour in the uplands of his heart.

He had dug no grave; he had thought to survive.
He had nothing to give; he had less to receive.
Objects avoided him, animals lied to him,
the Diamond Sutra hung, untranslatable, on his wall.

It was only then that he crept back in
and stole hunger and shaped it into
a bowl, in which, to this day, when no one
is looking, and the wind isn't blowing, he bathes.

Douceur d'être et de n'être pas
    – Paul Valéry

Her footfalls, born of his voicelessness,
paving their way, like a saint's steps, patiently
lead, wind-chilled and mute,
toward the watchman's bed.

Shoeless like the gods, and the long light
laid across her arms.
All the words, all the silences disguised as words,
adrift between us and the unsaid.

Finally her lips close in, the invisible
nutrition of the kiss
opening the dark bouquet of mouths
wadded into his head.

Take your time. He has always been there
waiting, and his heart out stalking, still
when you are still and moving as you move,
matching your stride, echoing your tread.

… der da mit seinem Schatten / getränktes liest
    – Rainer Maria Rilke

Who reads her while she reads? Her eyes slide
under the paper, into another world
while all we hear of it
or see is the slow surf of turning pages.

Her mother might not recognize her,
soaked to the skin as she is in her own shadow.
How could you then? You with your watch and tongue
still running, tell me: how much does she lose

when she looks up? When she lifts
the ladles of her eyes, how much
flows back into the book, and how much
spills down the walls of the overflowing world?

Children, playing alone, will sometimes
come back suddenly, seeing what it is
to be here, and their eyes are altered. Hers too. Words
she's never said reshape her lips forever.

Miesiąc jak królik wśród obłoków hyca
   – Jarosław Iwaszkiewicz

The moon sneaks like a rabbit from cloud to cloud.
In the darkness you can't see the funerals.
The light – no matter how little or much
we are given – spills down our cheeks,
though a portion is eaten each day
by our eyes, to feed the inedible
fruits of our voices.

Nevertheless, that moon up there
scares me. Some days it's priestly. I think it may
visit me one day, any day, shaped
like a boy.

The gods and the stars are all flying away.
Does anyone still think anything really
remains here? You're leaving too, I guess,
are you? Already?

Listen in simple words
to what I say. I know I sometimes
speak it, like an educated
foreigner, a little too
clearly. Even so, it is
your own tongue – which no one
anywhere may ever speak to you again.

Parfois l'air se contracte / Jusqu'à prendre figure
   – Jules Supervielle

Ravenous giraffes, you
star-lickers, steers
seeking the infinite in
a movement of the grass,

greyhounds out to catch it
on the run, roots
who know that it is
hidden down there somewhere:

what has it turned into
in me now that I am no more
than alive and all my handholds
are transparent sand?

The air contracts like something
taking form, but there is nothing
one can't kill if one is willing
to keep moving. Earthly

recollections, tell me
how to speak
with trees, with sea-waves
breaking, with a sleeping child. This

is what I wanted: just
to pacify my long-faced
memory, to tell it
a more patient story.

debo reanudar mis huesos en tu reino
        – Pablo Neruda

A man with no hands is still singing.
A bird with no hands is asking the world,
and the world is answering every day:
earth is the only flesh of the song.

A man with no wings is crossing
the sky's black rapids on his hands.
His mother's bones lie slumped
by the stumps of the cedars.

I carry my own bones in my hands
into your country,
and there are no kings; it is not a kingdom;
and there is no legend; it is the land
and a woman's body, and these are my bones.
What do I owe to these strangers my brothers?

☐ THEIR NAMES

Paradoxalement c'est la mort elle-même, décidant pour l'éternité, qui à jamais nous sauve de l'inexistence.... Celui qui a été ne peut plus désormais ne pas avoir été.... Tout est perdu, tout est donc sauvé.

Vladimir Jankélévitch
L'Irréversible et la nostalgie

The heart is a white mountain
left of centre in the world.
The heart is dust. The heart is trees.
The heart is snowbound broken
rock in the locked ribs of a man
in the sun on the shore of the sea who is dreaming
sun on the snow, dreaming snow on the broken
rock, dreaming wind, dreaming winter.

The heart is a house with torn floorboards.
The heart is a seeded and peeled
grape on the vine, a bell
full of darkness and anvils.
The heart is a flute with four fingerholes
played in the rain.
The heart is a deep well dug upward.

The heart is a sandstone canyon in the high
Triassic fields, inhabited by grass,
potsherds and scapulae, femurs and burnt corn,
with horned men and mountain sheep
painted and pecked on the straw-coloured walls.

The heart is three bowls
always full and one empty.
The heart is a four-winged
moth as it lifts and unfolds.
The heart is a full set of goat prints,
a pocket of unfired clay and a stray
piece of oatgrass:
two fossils: one locket;
a drenched bird squawking from the perch
in its overstuffed cage.

The heart is a deepwater sponge
tied up with smooth muscle in two
double half-hitches, sopping up blood
and twice every second wrung out like a rag.

The heart is a grave
waking, a corpse walking, a tomb
like a winter well-house, pulsing
with blood under the wilted noise
of the voices. The heart is a cut root
brooding in the worn earth,
limping, when no one is watching,
back into the ground.

The heart is four hands serving soup
made of live meat and water.
The heart is a place. The heart
is an unmentioned name.

The heart is everything, but nothing
is the heart. The heart is lime and dung and diapers
in a hole. The heart is wood. The heart is
diamond and cooked turnip, lead and precious metal,
stone. The heart is light. The heart is cold.

The heart is a smoking saxophone rolled
like a brass cigar in a mouth
like the mouth of Ben Webster,
something perforated, folded,
always emptying and filling,
something linking aching air
and a wet, shaking reed.

The heart is four unintersecting
strokes of the brush in Chinese,
with these homophones:

daylight, zinc, firewood, bitterness, joy,
earthbreath and *lampwicking,*
up which the blood is continually rising.

The heart is a pitcher of untasted water.

The heart is a white mountain
which the woman in the moon,
her left breast full of cellos and her right
breast full of violins,
climbs and is sometimes carried
up and down.

The heart is found
in the leaking bucket of the ribs,
in the distant hills, in the lover's
body, the belly, the mouth,
in the empty wheel between the knees.

The heart is being
knowing only that it is;
the heart is dumb; the heart is glass.

The heart is dust
trees locket rock sponge
house flute bell rain

The heart is being aching, being
beating, being knowing being
that not what not
who not how not why
it is the beating that it is.

1

Knowing, not owning.
Praise of what is,
not of what flatters us
into mere pleasure.

Earth speaking earth,
singing water and air,
audible everywhere
there is no one to listen.

2

Knowing, not owning:
being, not having,
the rags and the blisters
of knowledge we have:

touching the known
and not owning it. Holding
and held by the known,
and released and releasing,

becoming unknowing.
Touching and being
unknowing and knowing,
known and unknown.

3

Sharpening, honing
pieces of knowledge,
pieces of earth,
and unearthing the knowledge

and planting the knowledge
again. Question
and answer together
inhabit the ground.

This is our offering:
hunger, not anger,
wonder, not terror,
desire, not greed.

Knowing, not owning
the touch of another,
the other's reluctance,
the incense of fear;

the smell of the horses
in darkness, the thread
of the story, the thread
of the thread of the story;

arrowhead, bowstring,
snare; the breath
going out, the breath
going all the way out

and half-turning
and waiting there, listening.
Yes. Breath
that is lifted and carried

and entered and left.
Through the doorway of flesh,
the barely invisible
footprints of air.

4

Killing and eating
the four-footed gods
and the winged and the rooted,
the footless and one-footed

gods: making flesh
of their flesh, thought
from their thought in the form
of the traces they leave,

words from their voices,
music and jewellery
out of their bones,
dreams from their dances,

begging forgiveness,
begging continuance,
begging continuance and forgiveness
from the stones.

RUBUS URSINUS:
A PRAYER FOR THE BLACKBERRY HARVEST

Reaching through thorns,
milking the black
udders with stung
wrists. Sister and
mother and un-
named stranger, say:
whose is this dark
blood on my hands?

KOL NIDRE

Forgive me my promises. Those I have kept
and those I have broken. Forgive me
my pledges, my vows and the rest
of my boasts and concessions.

Raking my father's bones out of the long furnace, I knew
that what is is what links us. The ground
we all walk on, air we all breathe;
the rocks and trees that look down on us all in their candour –

all that remains of all that surrounded us when we were sane –
and the eyes; the hands; the silence; reciting the names
of what is in the world; divining the names
of what isn't; the wounds we inflict

to relay and mirror the wounds we receive;
and the knots that we cannot undo
between father and son, daughter and mother,
mother and father, the one

God and all his believers:
the marriage made without vows
between those who have pleased
and hurt one another that deeply.

FOR THE BONES OF JOSEPH MENGELE, DISINTERRED JUNE 1985

Master of Auschwitz, angel of death,
murderer, deep in Brazil they are breaking
your bones – or somebody's bones: my
bones, your bones, his bones, whose
bones does not matter. Deep in Brazil they are breaking
bones like loaves of old bread. The angel
of death is not drowning but eating.

Speak! they are saying. *Speak! speak!*
If you don't speak we will open and read you!
Something you too might have said in your time.
Are these bones guilty? they say. And the bones
are already talking. The bones, with guns
to their heads, are already saying, *Yes!*
Yes! It is true, we are guilty!

Butcher, baker, lampshade and candlestick
maker: yes, it is true. But the bones? The bones,
earth, metals, teeth, the body?
These are not guilty. The minds of the dead

are not to be found in the bones of the dead.
The minds of the dead are not anywhere to be found,
outside the minds of the living.

FATHERS AND SONS

for Jan Conn

I remember the face:
the mouth crouched in the silence, the eyes
bright as ripe olives, slippery as stones
in the sunlit creek bed, and suddenly
lightless as ash.

I remember
the taste of his voice, not the sound.
It was wet, salt, warm,
and it sat in my own throat, not in his,
like a mouthful of tears.

I remember him
yelling my name, and no more. My father
outlived me. There was a light and I reached for it. He
touched the air's cheek. Touched it
and floated there. Soared.

I suppose
he told everyone, later, how well
he had warned me and coached me, but nobody
coached me. No one said anything then.
Not to me.

We were locked
in a tall box canyon then, with that halfbreed
thing he had sired or midwived – which was it? –
that no one, not even my father,
could talk to.

I watched him.
I listened. He talked
to the rocks and the trees,
the bees and the hawks, not to me. But he gave me
the wings.

And for this, for a moment, I loathed
and revered him.

HICK & NILLIE

— Poet, said the god, Is this the truth?
— All words are true, the poet said.
                              — All words?
   the god said.
              — All words, said the poet.
— Lies are also true then, said the god.
— They are, the poet said. All words
   are empty, useless, placeless, true.
— Some words have places, said the god.
— Many words have places, said the poet.
— Are those with places empty? asked the god.
— Not if they're in place, the poet said.
— But you said....
              — Yes.
                     — You lied.
                            — I also

told the truth, the poet said.
All words are true, the truth is true,
and lies are also true. And you
and I stand eye-deep in our words.
— Deeper, I think, in your case, said the god.
— You do not think, the poet said.
— You're dead, the god said.
                              — Truly,
if you say so, said the poet.
Just as, if I say so, you're alive.
— I am and I am not alive, the god said.
This has nothing to do with you.
— Yes. Nevertheless, all words are true.
— None truer than others? asked the god.
— Words become less true with repetition,
even by a god.
                    — And less true still,
with repetition by a poet.
— Yes. All words were true in the beginning,
but all words now are less true, and a time
will come when all words will be false.
— What happens then? the god said.
— Speech will happen only in
the spaces that remain between the words.
— But speech is action, said the god.
— When words turn false, all acts
will do the same, the poet said.
— And then?
                    — The gods will stop. The poets
will grow silent, or turn vicious,
or turn coy.
                    — Not coyer than this?
                                        — Yes.
— Then what?
                    — Silence, like clear speaking,
washes words. In time they will
come true again. But then, of course,

they will be different words.
                              — How long
will all this take? the god asked.
— Moments, said the poet.
                              — Moments?
— Less than the time it takes to speak a word.

DEMONS AND MEN

Hepburn to Bogart, descending the river:
"Nature, Mr Alnutt,
is what we are put in the world
to rise above."

Herakleitos to Artemis,
leaving a fraying brick of chicken-scratched
papyrus on the sunlit polished stone:
ἦθος ἀνθρώπου δαίμων –
"habituation is a demon" – meaning
nothing to do with devils or damnation;
meaning nothing to do with sin, for which
there is no word in Herakleitos' language.

Meaning, "everybody's culture, custom, manner –
her identity, his ethos – is a minor, mortal god."
And meaning *how you do* is someone other.
He or she, not you, is who you are.
Meaning each of us is both
a being and a character,
a person and the armour that it wears.
You are you and not you.
A is A and not A.
I is not reducible to I.

And in the sea-blue sky
above the sky-blue sea, the still,
dry lightning of the pine branch
and the migratory jewel of the evening star.
Beneath the pine,
the thinning smell of sheep and lupine,
and the day's heat seeping from the stone.

Herakleitos, looking out across the river
in the shrinking sunlight, thinks
the silt is rising in the river as the pine forest falls.
Looking out across the river,
he mutters to his daughter:
ἦθος γὰρ ἀνθρώπειον μὲν οὐκ ἔχει
γνώμας, θεῖον δὲ ἔχει –
  "human culture has no purchase on what is,
but god-culture does."

— Purchase? says his daughter.

— Touch is the condensation of vision,
    Herakleitos says. The mind
    is a string-game played
    with fingers, ears and eyes.

— You used to say the brain
    is a swollen nose, his daughter answers.

— And I will again tomorrow.

— Couldn't they teach us? asks his daughter.

— Who?

— The gods.

— Thought starts from scratch each day, says Herakleitos,
  and the fallers start wherever they left off.
  Thought starts from scratch.
  Understanding starts from scratch.
  And the truth will save itself instead of you.

— In the city last week I saw a film,
  says Herakleitos' daughter.

— What did it say? asks Herakleitos.

— Two empires fought, and one of them won.
  The jungle was thick, and the river survived.
  But the missionary married the mechanic.
  After that, who knows?

THE FLOWERS OF THE BODY

1

We are the flowers we bring
to one another: two bouquets
of changing colours.
I count seven flowers,
flowering in layers.

The first is a flower the colour of earth,
in which the other flowers flower.
The second is all the colours of bone and
cornstraw, chlorophyll and blood.
The third is flame. The fourth
is turquoise, ochre, jade.
The fifth shifts like the mountain sky

or the sea from rose to indigo. The sixth
is the colourless colour of water and air.
And there is one more, rainbow-coloured like the deer.

2

Their common names are smell, taste,
sight, touch, sound, thought.
That is the end of the list. The last,
whose common name is silent, is
the one sense these lead from and toward.

3

These are the flowers of the body:
the nose at the base of the body;
the lips and tongue at the root of the body;
the eye looking out from the palm of the body;
the drum of the blood, strummed by the hand
that roosts like a bird in the heart of the body;
the ear in the pit of the throat, which is
the midpoint of the skin; the brain
in its leaking chalice of bone; the moon.

4

In the fist of the face, the flowers
reappear: nose, lips, eyes, ears.
The blossoms open, close, reopen,
reading and writing the light
on tattered scraps of air.
Behind the mind's back,
deep in the cloak of the body,
the blind roots listen through their pores,
squeezed in the face's other hand.

5

Ankles, elbows, shoulders, hips
and fingertips are the flowers sprouting
again in the slender bodies of arms and legs,
and again in the blinded faces of feet and hands.

6

The voices of the flowers of the body are
the voices of the stars, the sea,
the sea air, deep-sea ores,
the sounds below the throat,
for which there are no letters.

Eyes, hands, tongues can become
the flowers again and again but cannot
turn to pick and dry them. In their voices
we are spoken. They are silent
in the tongues in which we try to write them down.

7

We are the trees we plant
in the one earth of one another,
that they flower there
together: flowers we bring on the living
branch to one another,
uncut, rooted
in the darkness where there are
no other faces, shapes or colours,
no bouquets, no other
others,
and in spite of that,
all others,
and in spite of that,
no faces, voices, colours,

no bouquets,
no bringing,
no song singing itself
in the fingertips,
no tongues, no teeth,
no taut lips softening,
no opening
and closing, no
unsoftening,
no thought
of light and fire and
no fire
and no flowers
and no hands.

SUNDAY MORNING

for Don McKay & Jan Zwicky

Moonset at sunrise, the mind
dividing between them. The teeth
of the young sun sink through the breast of the cloud.
And a great white pelican rests in the bay,
on his way from Great Slave Lake
to Guatemala.
The mind is made out of the animals
it has attended.
In all the unspoken languages,
it is their names.
Mule deer, black bear, killer whale, salmon.

To know means to hold no opinions: to know
meaning thinks, thinking means.
The mind is the place not already taken.
The mind is not-yet-gathered beads of water
in the teeth of certain leaves –
Saxifraga punctata, close by the stream
under the ridge leading south to Mount Hozameen,
for example – and the changing answers of the moon.
The mind is light rain gathered
on the ice-scarred rock, a crumpled mirror.

To be is to speak with the bristlecone
pines and the whitebarks,
glaciers and rivers, grasses and schists,
and if it is permitted, once also
with pelicans. Being
is what there is room for in that
conversation. The loved is what stays
in the mind; that is, it has meaning,
and meaning keeps going. This
is the definition of meaning.

What is is not speech.
What is is the line
between the unspeakable
and the already spoken.

☐ THE BLUE ROOFS OF JAPAN

A Duet for Interpenetrating Voices

for Audrey Thomas,
in whose voice it all began

This is a poem for male and female speaking voice. The woman's voice, which starts the poem and steers it, is set in indented italics. For the sake of legibility, the voices appear to alternate on the page. In fact, they must speak together:

> *Woman's voice alone.*

Man's voice speaking

> *And the woman's voice speaking*

while the woman speaks too.

> *at the same time.*

Man's voice alone.

A performance score, with the two voices superimposed, printed in two colours, appears in *Pieces of Map, Pieces of Music* (McClelland & Stewart, 1986; Copper Canyon Press, 1987).

I

        In a house with
In a house with such a blue
        such a blue
roof, she said with red
        roof, you'd wake up cheerful
hair, you'd wake up cheerful
        every morning.
every morning.

        To the talking mirror
To the talking mirror
        of water,
of water. To the broken panes
        to the talking mirror
of water laid in the earth like leaded glass.
        of water.

To the empty cup containing
        To
everything,
        the cup containing
to warm it with the tea.
        everything, the hands

To hold in the hands like a cup of tea,
always full and always empty,
        always empty, always full.
the earthy asymmetry of the world.

To the rich, disordered earth,
        To the order of the earth.
to the sound of mountain water,

to the boundless

       To the boundless –

truth of the ground.

       not infinite, boundless –
       truth of the ground.

To the world with its welcome
imperfections.

               Violence hides

Violence hides in fastidious order.

       under the lid of fastidious order.

To the polished lacquer
platter where the drunken
lion grins.

And to the knowledge it is June; the moon

       The moon

is choking on its own light; the river

       is swelling. Violence hides.

fish are running; at Gifu the leashed
cormorants dive.

To the water that walks over stones

       The water walks

through the long wooden town

       over stones through the long

like a roshi on wide wooden slippers:

       wooden town.

the river marched through the Chinese grid

       The river is marched through the Chinese grid

of the city, not twisting but turning,

       of the city,

as sharp as a section-line road
                     as sharp
through the Saskatchewan prairie.
                as a section-line road
                through the prairie.

To the Sleeping Dragon
                To
Garden: to the wordless speech of water
                the water. To the water.
broached in the silence of the stone.
                To the stone.

To the spoken
shakuhachi, its calligraphy
                    To the speaking,
of sound.
                to the silence,
To the trees –
                to the trees –
karamatsu, gingko, sugi, bamboo –
                karamatsu,
who speak for themselves; to the emperor's
                gingko, sugi, bamboo;
bound and housebroken pines.

To knowing the Emperor's carp and his wood ducks
                karamatsu,
are pretty, but they are not his,
                gingko, sugi, bamboo.
and his roof is dark brown.
                But the Emperor's
                roof is dark brown.

This music is all about water,
>   *This music is water, this water*
she said. How the hollowed wood
>   *is music:*
redistributes the air:
>   *the hollow bamboo*
ruffled or clear, how the breath
>   *redistributes the water.*
descends: how it pools and pours
>   *The air, like the water, descends.*

through the holes in the voice,
through the joints in the body, the stem
of bamboo, through the discontinuities
in the skeleton, knots in the plank
>   *In the unbroken muscle of water,*
at the annual branching: nodes
>   *the wholeness of bone,*
of nonbeing: not breath but the silences
>   *is the sudden*
>   *completeness*
between breathing: these
>   *of being*
are the song; the rest
is just singing.
>   *the singing.*

Writing is planting.
Writing is born in the lands of wet-farming.
The field prefigures the table and page.
The garden prefigures the table and page.

> *Is a woman's body*
> *the garden?*

Writing derives

> *Writing descends*

from the domestication of water.
Rain and the sea

> *like the rain on the sea.*

are the mothers of letters.

> *Rain and the sea*

The mind of the scribe

> *are the mothers of letters.*

moves like a long-legged waterbird,
stoops like a rice-farmer, steps like a crane.

> *Rain and the sea are the mothers of letters.*

When you next see the hunters,
say to the hunters:
O say can you see

> *Can you see?*

how the earth is rewritten

> *Can you see how the earth is re-*

under our hands

> *written?*

until it says nothing?

Say to the hunters: The herders
have taught us the meters, but we

> *The herders have taught us*

have forgotten. Say to the hunters:
                    the meters, but we
                    have forgotten.
Teach us a song

                    Say to the hunters:
as subtle as speaking, teach us
                    The mothers of rhythms
a song as lean and as changeable
                    are rain and the sea.
as the world.

IV

But who was it who taught us
the artist's ambitions:
a house in the country, a house
in the town, an apartment in history?

Listen: this music
is all about water. The words
                    this music too
are the earth, and the music
                    this music too
is water.

An artist is anyone
who remembers, it is not you nor me
                    anyone who
nor the boss but the gods who are watching.
                    anyone who
For these we perform. The others
are eavesdroppers, boob-squeezers, thieves
or voyeurs, or they work here.

The tongues of the gods include
no dates and no names.
This is the logos.
                    THIS *is*
                    the logos.

V

All afternoon, the slow
celebration of these
     This music is water;
two equations:
earth plus water plus fire
      this laughter is fire.
gives earth that holds water;
water plus fire plus leaf
     Water plus fire
gives a bowl full of tea.
    plus leaf

A gesture, a form within matter
     recentres the air.
recentres the air.

    Neither counting nor naming.

Earthsong and seasong, they say:
the native and foreign.

    Naming, not counting.

Water and earth: what ties us together
holds us apart.
     What holds us apart
     is what ties us together.

The mountains are younger than birds.
The sea when we lived in the sea
was made of fresh water.
No man is not one of these islands.

What ties us to time and the world
beside us is fire.

Counting, not naming.

Water is wordless, while the earth
is information. Earth is words.
This too is the logos. A journey on foot
cannot be repeated, just as a story
cannot be recited, only retold.

Naming and counting.

Facing the water, be music.
Be still facing fire.
                    Be laughter.
Be laughter.
                    One. Two. Three.
Facing the earth, be darkness.
                    Four.
Facing the sky, be quiet, wide and blue.
                    Five.

☐ NEW WORLD SUITE Nº 3

Four Movements for Three Voices

1 **First voice (male) in bold.**

Second voice (female) in italic.

Third voice (male) in roman.

2 **The lines in each stave are spoken simultaneously.**

These three lines are spoken simultaneously.

Sometimes, in other words, we all talk at once.

3 **But these   in sequence.**

      three   speak

          voices

moderato

1 **What is is what has happened, Hegel says,**

_____

_____

                                        Who cares

_____

2 **and what has happened is what is**

_____

_____

what Hegel says? What happens is what is.

_____

3   **spread out through time.**

_____

What is is what is timeless caught in time.

_____

_____

4   **They were coming**

_____

Farmers and shopkeepers, slavers and Quakers, they came,

_____

Workers and freeloaders, thieves

_____

5 **like sprung prisoners,**

beating the tongues

and policemen, they came,

6

of their women out into wagon sprags,

and keep coming.

7   **beating their own ears**

axeheads and spades. The rhythms

8 **into ploughshares.**

of history are the rhythms

It is written that history

9

of buying and selling, obeying

is the saviour of nature, time

10   **What is there,**

and forcing, instead of the rhythms

the saviour of space.

11 **in that case, to sing of?**

of giving and bearing.

If that is the case,

12 **What is there to hear?**

Which shall we listen for?

what is there to listen for, or to sing of?

13 **Fleeing Copernicus, fleeing from Galileo they came,**

Fleeing, not seeing,

They were running away. What they ran from

14 **refusing the news that what is**

refusing, not choosing, they came –

came with them.

15   is bigger than history. Time

though some of them chose, and still choose,

               And when they arrived,

16   is the earth and the sky turning imperfect circles,

to believe they are chosen.

            they kept running.

17   not God on his tall parade to the end of the line.

      Time is the sky and the earth, dancing.

• • • • • • • • •

18

At Cuzco, Tenochtitlan, Acoma, Kitwancool,

19   Cuzco, Tenochtitlan, Acoma,

the churches squat on the ruins.

20 **Kitwancool.**

At Pisaq and Tikal, Chaco Canyon, Tanu ...

21 **Pisaq and Tikal, Chaco**

Visitors gnaw at the moth-eaten light

22 **Canyon, Tanu.**

at Frijoles and Gila ...

with mechanical eyes.

23 **Frijoles and Gila.**

Gila, Frijoles ...

Whole towns are trussed up in the webs

24

whole towns ...

of our fences and parking lots,

25

Tikal and Pisaq…

guardrails, turnstiles, interpretive signs.

26 **The truth predigested in place, like a caught**

Tenochtitlan, Acoma…

       The truth is broken like bread

27 **moth, through the alchemical weight of our hands.**

Cuzco… Tanu… Kitwancool…

in our hands.

28 **In Denver…   Los Angeles…   Vancouver…**

      in Toronto…   in Boston…

29 **the motorized spirochetes move on their cancerous business,**

the living are dead and the dead pretend

30 **the tumours of asphalt and neon enlarge.**

to be living.

    Hour by hour the tumours enlarge,

31   **They are beautiful, yes,**

and their beauty is visible from the aircraft,

32 **from the aircraft. The distance that brings**

                What is

like that of bacilli seen through the microscope in the lab.

33 **what we do into focus**

is what is timeless

The distance that brings what we do

34 **shrinks and increases,**

caught in time.

into focus shrinks

35 **our legs stay the same length, and the path**

and increases. Our legs stay the same length.

36 **from the kiva is empty.**

The roads between city and country are filled.

37

The way out and back from the vision

Black trails unroll through the hills.

38 **Sheetmetal thoroughbreds gleam at the curbside.**

is empty.

Suits of armour and horse-armour

39

Four-wheeled kachinas live year around in the town.

sleep in the house and feed at the table.

40 History here is a clock ticking, a blade

Therefore the deer remain dead,

41 sliding between the earth and our shoes.

        and the pronghorn are spooked by the fences.

. . . .

42 Up the Xingú and Uraricoera:

    The mother of rivers has thousands

    In the Amazon,

43 the ashes still warm and the blood still fresh

of rivers for mothers.

rivers go bankrupt. All over the world, the earth

44 in the logging slash, and the featureless mud

    What do the words

is tortured for money.

45 **of the goldfields pulped with a high-pressure hose.**

mean when we say them?

The pitmines

46

Homicide, genocide, fluvicide, terracide,

at Kimberley, Bingham and Cerro de Pasco;

47

at Alamogordo, the acres of radioactive glass.

48 **This is not history.**

matricide, parricide?

This is the whipped

49

earth already ceasing to whimper,

50   **In our presence**

Who can answer?

closing her mask.

51 the real is frequently speechless.

The real, in our presence, is speechless.

52   **What is is an idea**

What is is an idea recurrent in time

53 recurrent in time, not

and there is no end to it:

What is keeps repeating. What is

54 your apocalypse, not your jihad,

not your apocalypse, not your jihad,

is an idea recurrent in time.

55 **not Armageddon. What is is mortal**

and not Armageddon.

56 **but plural.**

What does that mean, Armageddon?

The death of what is is the wet dream

57

Not your apocalypse, not your jihad.

of impotent men and of overdosed children,

58   **The dreamers**

Looking for birth,

starved for the sight of the bright knife of the world,

59 **who dream of the end of the world have never**

touching death, and unsure of the difference,

shouting *kapow!*

194

60 **sat down face to face with the world.**

parents and children are playing.

and greening their knees on the manicured lawn.

. . . .

61

At Gods' Narrows the children

62

play tag in the ditches, dodging the corpses

In Brazil... Indonesia... in the Philippines...

63   **At Gods' Narrows**

of dogs and the used plastic diapers

Chile...   Ontario...   Manitoba...

64 **the children play tag in the ditches.**

and kleenex and kotex and broken machines.

the limbs and the stumps

65 **Their food has come 2000 miles in bottles and cans.**

Our bread, the colour

of people and trees.

66

and odour of old snow,

Their songs

67

has come 500 miles in cellophane.

come to them weekly on tape from Tennessee.

68 **What stories they have have been brought in a book**

Stories are fed to them

69 **from a place without caribou, moose, wolf, lynx.**

from a book.

70

Without whiskeyjack, black spruce, beaver or bear.

They are taught to call it the Holy Book.

71 **They are taught to call it the Holy Land.**

72

Weaned from the earth, we are fed

73 **Weaned from the earth, they are fed**

on the eggwhite and sugar of visions

Weaned

74 **on the sugar of other men's dreams.**

of life after death in a different world,

from the earth, they are fed

75

not on the meat of the knowledge that this

on dead words.

76   **I do not know how many**

is that different world.

77 **worlds, past, present and future, exist.**

                              How many worlds?

          Are there many worlds?

78 **I know there are many.**

With how many faces?

                    I know,

79

And how many trees,

nevertheless, there is no other world

80

full of how many voices?

than this, with its different faces, its trees

81   **What is is not what we have built;**

The fear of death

full of voices, its eyes like trap doors.

82 **it is what we have not yet found time**

is deadly.

There is no other world.

83 **to destroy.**

This hunger for life everlasting

84   **This hunger for life**

will kill us.

We know this and ought not to care

85 everlasting will kill us. And kill

for ourselves, though it is hard not to think

86 many others. Trout, mountain hemlock,

But what of the others?

of the others.

87 deermice, deer.

Something will be here.

88 Being will be here.

Beauty will be here.

89 But this beauty that visits us now will be gone.

This beauty, like all beauty,

Being will be here.

90

is mortal, but beauty will be here.

The deer are as violent with trees

91

We are one, even though

as wolves with the deer, and the number of beings

92   **The number of ideas of being**

we are many.

is many.

93 is many, though not beyond counting.

The size of the heart

94   **The size of the mind**

is the number of creatures.

The size of the heart is the number of creatures.

95 is the number of species of creatures.

The size of the mind is the number

96   And I do not know how to measure

of species of creatures.

97 the depth and extent of what is in the world,

What we cannot see must be

98 but I think that when counting the gods, zero and one

equally many.

How many gods can you name? That is the size

99   are two answers equally useless.

Zero and one are two instants, two gifts, not two answers.

of your view of the world.

. . . .

100 What is is an idea recurrent in time.

What is is an idea, yes,

What is

101   There are no blueprints

but what is is right here.

is recurrent in time. Descriptions

102   or duplicates elsewhere.

and photographs will not do for rebuilding the world.

103   The songs are not maps,

The stories are maps.

The stories are maps.

104 they are caches and trails.

Song is edible

The songs are not maps,

105   **The singers**

thought but not seedgrain.

they are caches and trails.

106 **bring in the hands of their voices**

The singers bring

Song is edible

107 **thought like dried meat**

in the hands of their voices

thought, but not

108 **and thought like the light it is given**

thought like dried meat

seedgrain. The singers bring

109 **by water and oil.**

and thought like the light

in the hands of their voices

I return to the earth's lap

it is given by water and oil.

thought like dried meat,

111 **all that remains of all she has given me: meals**

I too must return to the earth's lap, with all

and thought like the light it is given

112 **for the eye, the belly, the hand – and what held them:**

she has given me. Even my children are hers.

by water and oil.

113 **ruined meat,**

The mind like a mildewed jewel,

114 **the crazy panpipes of the bones**

muscles and bones

115   that sang when certain women touched me

crazy for women, crazy for sunlight,

116   and when I touched the world.

and eyes crazy for water, trees and stones.

· · · · · · · · · ·

117

The children of those who cross over

118   **Their children's children**

the water must wander.

        The children of those

119   must swim through the ground.

        Their children's children

who cross over the water

must swim through the ground.

must wander. Their children's

121 **I set out to listen for.**

But there is a song I thought you should hear,

children must swim through the ground.

122

and a story that tells where to find it.

I thought I remembered a song and a story.

123 **Year after year the song sinks deeper**

I thought you should hear it.

124 **under the seacliffs. Year after year**

The song has gone under the seacliffs.

The song has gone under the sea.

125 **it sings itself farther back into the hills.**

Year after year it sings itself farther

And year after year

126 **And the hills dance,**

under the mountain. And year after year

it sings itself farther back into the hills.

127 **but only when no one**

we dance it back out again.

And the hills dance

128 **is looking.**

If the hills dance, we dance too.

only so long as no one is watching.

andante

1

The healers dream in the eastern mountains.

2 The lords of the mountains go there to die.

3

It is silent, except for the bluegreen songs of the birds.

4 Dead mountain sheep, people, pronghorn and deer

When they are dead, mountain sheep,

5 dance in their white masks on the polished floors

people, pronghorn and deer

6 of the western lakes.

Their steps are wet and slow.

dance on the lakefloor.

7 Four storeys up are the homes of the birds.

The homes of the birds are four storeys up.

8

Four storeys up are the homes of the birds.

The roots of the trees are four storeys down.

9 In the four directions are oceans.

Four storeys down

Poisons

10

are the trees' roots.

percolate into them all.

11

The earth was married to the sky,

The healers dream in the eastern

12 **The earth was married to the sky,**

but he was cold, and so she left him.

mountains. The lords of the mountains

13 **but he was cold.**

She lives now with the sea.

go there to die.

14

Her sons and her daughters, by both these fathers,

It is silent, except for the bluegreen

15   **Persons are cooked, and persons are raw.**

are persons.

songs of the birds.

16 **Cooked persons keep their forms**

Daylight cooks us,

                    Dead

17 **and uncooked persons change them.**

little by little, day by day.

mountain sheep, pronghorn and deer

18 **Deer, bear, douglas-fir, the earth, the sun**

              You are cooked, but deer, bear,

dance in their white masks

19 **and snowstorms, for example, all have roots**

douglas-fir, the earth, the sun

on the polished floors of the western lakes.

20   in the cool darkness. They stay raw.

     and snowstorms all stay raw.

                    Their steps are wet and slow.

       • • • • • • • • •

21   In the sky is a knife made of stone with no handle.

                    It flies

22

  like a bird.

  The heart of the knife

23   The morning star is its eye.

  is the evening star.

24   The heart of the earth is not in the sky.

               The earth's heart beats

          In the sky is a knife made of stone

25 **The eye of the earth is open,**

in the motionless stone.

with no handle. It flies like a bird.

26 **but it is hidden.**

Thought is light.

The heart of the knife

27 **The darkness is thinking.**

The world's thought is called the sun.

is the evening star,

28 **Behind the earth's back, hiding from thought**

beating, not blinking.

29 **under rocks, in the roots and leaves**

Thought is light.

The morning star is its eye.

30 **of trees, is thinking.**

      The darkness is thinking.

31   **What**

  These are the chief equations describing the motions

32 **is it thinking?**

                             In summer at sunrise:

  linking the heart and thought of the world.

33 **Magpie.**   **Wolf.**

      Whitetail.

          Cottonwood.

34   **Mule deer.**

  In summer at sunset: Oriole.

          Ponderosa.   Cougar.

35   **Pronghorn.**   **Aspen.**

In winter at sunrise:

                              Bobcat.   And macaw.

36   **Douglas-fir?**   **The mountain**

In winter at sunset:

                              Steller's jay.

37   **sheep?**

The world's thought is called

          [*laughs*] Coyote.

38 **The sun is married to the moon. He doesn't touch her.**

          the sun.

              These are the chief equations describing the motions

39

Salt is his elder sister. His grandmother lives

linking the heart and thought of the world.

40

in a blue house near a dark beach littered with shells.

In summer at sunrise:

41 **He visits her there at evening in midwinter.**

magpie, whitetail, cottonwood, wolf.

42

He visits her there in midsummer at dawn.

In summer at sunset:

43 **His sons are the clown, who comes in summer,**

ponderosa, oriole, mule deer, cougar.

44 **and the twins, who come in winter.**

It is two to one,

In winter at sunrise: pronghorn,

45

and the clown is a hunchback, but he is clever.

bobcat, aspen and macaw.

46 **The twins are gamblers and soldiers.**

In winter at sunset:

47

The clown of summer discovered the flute,

douglas-fir,

48

and he is the raw person whose picture you see

the Steller's jay,

49

on the face of the motionless stone

the mountain sheep,

where the heart of the earth beats.

[*laughs*] coyote.

51 **There he is playing his flute, and like it or not,**

Because he is there, playing

52 **here we are dancing.**

There he is playing his flute, and here we are dancing.

his flute, we are here, dancing.

adagio

1

Snowcloud, darkness, snow.

2 **What is not is not hidden.**

What is

What?

3

is not hidden, although it is hiding.

4 **The truth is, there is no horizon.**

The truth is one thing.

The sky

5 **Snow and more snow.**

and the earth, like the truth, are one thing.

6

Add us also, the sum is still smaller than two.

Snow and more snow.

7 **Watch your step.**

Watch your step, my grandfather said.

8

I watched you. You tripped,

And I did so and tripped, and he laughed.

9 **Not your foot, but your step.**

and he laughed.

Not your foot, but your step, he said.

10 **Nothing can stray. There is**

Nothing can stray.

11 **no way of leaving the path.**

Nothing can stray, he said.

There is no way of leaving the path.

12 **What you are is what is. It runs**

Nothing can stray.

What you are is what is, he said.

13 **all the way through. The grass**

It runs all the way through.

14 **and the stars are your innermost nature.**

I don't see any grass.

The snow underfoot and the stars

15

The gods come, unseen, to drink

in the sky are your nature.

16

at the thought's edge. Why,

Nothing

17   **Two emotions at once,**

where, and from whom could one hide?

can stray.

18 **three, even four –**

The stars in the sky

Two emotions at once, three, even four,

19 **each in due measure.**

and the snow underfoot

but each in due measure within you, he said.

20 **That is good order, of course,**

are the facts of the matter.

That is good order, my grandfather said.

21 **but a space without boundaries**

But the empty space

22 **surrounds them.**

What surrounds us is boundless, he said.

that surrounds those emotions

23 **And that space**

It is empty,

is it, he said.

24 **is the core.**

and that is the core.

That is the core.

lento

1 The sun burns to the ground and is kindled again,

The sun burns to the ground.

2 teaching the one lesson deeper than hunger.

It is kindled again. There is one lesson

3   In the night sky, Orion,

Orion, the old god, disguised as a deer, is out

deeper than hunger.

4 disguised as a deer, is out stalking Aldebaran,

stalking Aldebaran, the doe, his daughter, forever.

5 **the doe, his daughter, forever.**

Arcturus is spearing the Great Bear

Arcturus, spearing the Great Bear of heaven, sees

6

---

of heaven. He sees in her eyes, now and always,

---

in her eyes, now and always, the eyes of his mother.

---

7 **The stars and the darkness glide at one speed,**

---

the eyes of his mother.

The stars and the darkness

---

8 **going nowhere to everywhere, or the reverse, and returning.**

---

glide at one speed, going everywhere, nowhere, or both,

---

9   **The wolves speak**

The wolves speak to the moon on behalf of the mountain.

---

and returning.

---

10 to the moon on behalf of the mountain.

                                    Everywhere,

Year after year, we who have traded our voices for words

11 Year after year, we who have traded our voices

                        year after year,

circle back to the pool

12 for words circle back to the pool

we who have traded our voices for words

of alkaline silence

13 of alkaline silence to listen.

circle back to the pool of alkaline silence to listen.

to listen.

14   **The sun burns to the ground.**

The sun burns to the ground and is kindled again,

15 It is kindled again. There is one lesson

teaching the one lesson deeper than hunger.

16 deeper than hunger.

Orion, the old god, disguised as a deer, is out

In the night sky, Orion,

17

stalking Aldebaran, the doe, his daughter, forever.

disguised as a deer, is out stalking Aldebaran,

18 Arcturus, spearing the Great Bear of heaven, sees

Arcturus is spearing the Great Bear

the doe, his daughter, forever.

19 in her eyes, now and always, the eyes of his mother.

of heaven. He sees in her eyes, now and always,

the eyes of his mother.

The stars and the darkness glide at one speed,

21 glide at one speed, going everywhere, nowhere, or both,

going nowhere to everywhere, or the reverse, and returning.

22 and returning.

The wolves speak to the moon on behalf of the mountain.

The wolves speak

23 Year after year, we who have traded our voices for words

Everywhere, nowhere, reverse, and returning.

to the moon on behalf of the mountain.

24 circle back to the pool

Year after year,

Year after year, we who have traded our voices

25 of alkaline silence

we who have traded our voices for words

for words circle back to the pool

26   **to listen.**

circle back to the pool of alkaline silence to listen.

of alkaline silence to listen.

BǍIZHÀNG HUÁIHǍI (Pai-chang Huai-hai, 720–814) A Zen monk working in Jiangxi; author of the first set of Zen monastic rules.

BANKEI YŌTAKU (1622–1693) A Zen monk and Confucian scholar, born near Himeji, in southern Honshu.

BODHIDHARMA (*fl. c.* 500 AD?) A bug-eyed monk from southern India who immigrated to China, becoming the titular founder of Chinese Zen.

DÀHUÌ ZONGGǍO (Ta-hui Tsung-kao, 1089–1163) A Zen monk of the Rinzai school. His teacher was Yuánwǔ Kèqín, who edited the poems of Xuědòu to produce the *Blue Cliff Record*.

DANXIÁ ZǏCHÚN (*c.* 1065–*c.* 1119) 'Redcloud.' A Zen monk whose poems are collected in the *Xutáng Jí* or *Gathering in the Empty Room*.

DŌGEN (1200–1253) A Zen teacher born in Kyoto. He studied in China with Tiantóng Rújìng, then returned to Japan to found the monastery of Eiheiji on the northwest coast of Honshu.

DÒNGSHAN LIÁNGJIÈ (Tung-shan Liang-chieh, 807–869) A Zen teacher working in Jiangxi. The Cáodòng or Soto school of Zen is named for him and his student Cáoshan Běnjí.

EURYTOS (5th century BC?) A Presocratic thinker mentioned by Theophrastos and Aristotle. He tried, it seems, more literally than anyone before or since to picture the world in numerical terms.

FǍYǍN WÉNYÌ (Fa-yen Wen-i, 885–958) Founder of the short-lived Fǎyǎn school of Zen. He was born in Hangzhou and taught in Nanjing.

HÁN SHAN (*fl. c.* 800 AD) The hermit poet of Cold Mountain in the Tiantai Range, Zhejiang.

HIPPOLYTUS (*c.* 170–235) A Roman bishop. His book, *Philosophoumena,* traces a number of Christian heresies to Presocratic roots, thus preserving otherwise unavailable fragments of the early Greek philosophers.

JAKUSHITSU GENKŌ (1290–1367) A Zen monk, poet and hermit living in Okayama.

LÍNJÌ YÌXUÁN (Lin-chi I-hsuan, *c.* 800–867) A Zen teacher from Hebei, who founded the Línjì or Rinzai school.

JOSEPH MENGELE (1911–1979?) German physician in charge of medical experiments at Auschwitz-Birkenau. After the war, he was rumoured to be living in South America, then to have drowned near São Paulo. In 1985, a skeleton thought to be his was exhumed and exhaustively tested.

NĀGĀRJUNA (2nd century AD?) 'The White Serpent.' A dialectical philosopher who taught near Amarvati, on the Krishna River, in Andhra Pradesh.

PARŚVANĀTHA (*c.* 820–776 BC?) A North Indian sage, traditionally counted the 23rd patriarch of the Jains.

SARĀHA (8th century AD?) A philosopher-poet living in Bengal and writing in the Apabhraṃsa language.

SENGZHÀO (Seng-chao, 384–414) A Buddhist philosopher born in Shaanxi. He studied at Chang'an with the captive translator Kumarajiva.

TIANTÓNG RÚJÌNG (T'ien-t'ung Ju-ching, 1163–1228) A Zen monk of the Soto school who taught in Jiangsu and Zhejiang. Teacher of Dōgen.

TZUHALEM (*c.* 1795–1854) A Halkomelem Salish hunter from the Cowichan River country on the southeast coast of Vancouver Island. At his camp on the mountain now bearing his name, he accumulated a number of women – holding them captive, it is said, both by physical and by psychological means. In 1830 his tribal elders convicted him *in absentia* of bride-theft and murder. He was killed in December 1854 as he tried to kidnap yet another wife from one of the Gulf Islands.

BEN WEBSTER (1909–1973) One of the great tenor sax men. He was born in Kansas City and died in Amsterdam.

XUĚDÒU ZHÒNGXIǍN (Hsueh-tou Chung-hsien, 980–1052) 'Snowcave.' A Zen monk and poet in the tradition of Yúnmén. He compiled an anthology of koans, writing a short poem to accompany each. A century later a Rinzai monk named Yuánwǔ Kèqín – the teacher of Dàhuì Zonggǎo – edited the collection, adding a commentary and notes, to produce what is known as the *Bìyán Lù* or *Blue Cliff Record*.

YǑNGJIA XUÁNJUÉ (Yung-chia Hsuan-chueh, 665–713) A poet and monk little interested in monastic life. He spent, it is said, only one day with his teacher Huìnéng, then returned to his home on the Zhejiang coast where he wrote the *Zhèndào Ge* or *Song of the Path of the Evidence*.

YÚNMÉN WÉNYǍN (Yün-men Wen-yen, 864–949) A Zen teacher born near Shanghai. He taught in northern Guangdong.

YÚNYÁN TÁNSHÈNG (Yün-yen T'an-sheng, 780–841) 'Frowning Cloud.' The teacher of Dòngshan Liángjiè.

LǏ BÓ and ZHUANG ZI will be more familiar to some readers in the older spelling, as Li Po and Chuang Tzu.

Chant and verse are preservatives, but poems still evolve, in the reading and the speaking, just as stories do in the telling and plays in the staging. For a time at least, like sacked and weighed potatoes, written language remains alive. Some of these poems were in print as early as 1972, but in places the text has continued to change. Their original form, I imagine, is one they are still waiting for me to give them when I have learned to write well enough. Trial versions of some of the newer poems appeared in *Border Crossings* (Winnipeg), *Canadian Literature* (Vancouver), *Descant* (Toronto), *Ellipse* (Sherbrooke, Québec), *Margin* (London), *Poetry Canada* (Kingston, Ontario), *Windhorse Review* (Yarmouth, Nova Scotia), and in the anthologies *Soho Square III* (Bloomsbury Press, 1990), *Take This Waltz* (The Muses' Company, 1994), *Towards 2000* (Fifth House, 1991) and *Witness to Wilderness* (Arsenal Pulp Press, 1994).

I owe a great deal to the editors and publishers I have worked with in the past two decades. But books and magazines, useful though they are, are still where poems are stored, not where they thrive. I am grateful above all that many of these poems have been whispered, spoken and performed by others where my own lame voice could never have reached.

The sentence on page 116 is taken from the *Xuěmè lùn,* "Lecture on the Pulse," attributed to Bodhidharma: *yi qiè shí zhong dàn yǒu yǔ yán dào duàn jí shì zì xin,* "Right there, everywhere language doesn't reach, is where the mind is." In this tradition too, the spoken takes precedence over the written, and the unspeakable over the spoken.

I'm grateful to Crispin Elsted, Janet Downie and Brad Prevedoros, who rehearsed the *New World Suite* with me repeatedly, and to Stan Dragland, Don McKay, Tish Woodley and Jan Zwicky, who listened closely throughout for flaws in the text. Not least, I'm grateful to the Canada Council and the John Simon Guggenheim Memorial Foundation, whose help has meant much to me over the years.

Kay Amert led me to the house on the Quai aux Fleurs where Vladimir Jankélévitch lived until his death in 1983. His book on time and memory, quoted on page 150, is published by Flammarion, Paris, copyright © 1974 by Flammarion.

The cover painting is **Jack Shadbolt**'s
Requiem (1987; private collection),
cropped for this purpose by the artist
and used with his kind permission.

The typefaces used throughout
are Minion and Poetica, both
designed by Robert Slimbach
and issued by Adobe Systems,
Mountain View, California.
The Greek font is a prototype
version of Minion Greek, which has
not yet been publicly released.
It is used here through the courtesy
of Adobe Systems Incorporated and
the designer, Robert Slimbach.

Typography by Robert Bringhurst;
composition by Susanne Gilbert
at the Typeworks, Vancouver.

The Modern Canadian Poets Series presents the finest poetry of contemporary English Canada. Each volume is drawn from the work of a single writer, either at mid-career or after a lifetime's achievement. General editors for the series have been Dennis Lee, Russell Brown, Sam Solecki, and, as of 1993, Stan Dragland.

THE MODERN CANADIAN POETS SERIES
TITLES AVAILABLE

OTHER COLLECTIONS OF SELECTED POEMS AVAILABLE
FROM MCCLELLAND & STEWART: